I'M NOT GOING
TO LIE OVER ONE
PARTRIDGE

Hope you enjoy this
Ernie Nutting

I'm Not Going To Lie Over One Partridge

Ernie Nutting

Book and cover design: Neil Petrunia

ISBN 978-0-9920834-4-1 (print)
ISBN 978-0-9920834-5-8 (pdf)

Printed and bound in Canada

Published by Epix Design Inc.
37 Westridge Crescent
Okotoks, AB T1S 0G7
(403) 263-7025

Second Printing September 2018.
Third Printing April 2021.

Contents

LIVING THE DREAM

SUNDRE

This book is dedicated to the
memory of my nephew Braden.

"Members Only"

Introduction

Let's start! If your friends and family tell you, "You should write a book," chances are very good that you shouldn't, and stick with your day job. But like a line in a popular movie, "If someone calls you a horse – ignore him. If you are called a horse a second time, let it go. But if you are called a horse a third time maybe it's time to start shopping for a saddle."

This is not an exercise in blowing my own horn, or bragging, or settling scores – hopefully this will just simply be an enjoyable journey for you, the reader.

It's like this – a guy was standing in front of me at the Calgary Stampede. He had thick black hair and a buzz cut with a big bejesus scar. I asked him what the heck happened to you? He said he was up in the mountains on Sheep Creek resting in his tent with his head against the canvas. He got bumped by what he thought was his horse and he swatted back and in return was swatted back by a bear – scarring his head.

I relayed this story to my old friend Charlie and I said, "I don't know whether to believe him or not." Charlie replied, "Bear stories aren't to be believed or not believed – they're to be enjoyed." So please enjoy this.

Don't hold my feet to the fire over every detail or date – it's simply how I remember them. And I'm going to be mentioning a lot of names. None of them are you – I've changed every name to protect the innocent (and the guilty) – so get over it. It's like that Carly Simon song, "You're so vain, I bet you think this song is about you." I didn't even know Carly Simon knew me or why she would write a song about me!

I'll state a little about myself to help you understand more where this book is coming from. I am one of 13 kids: 11 boys and two girls raised on a mixed farm in rural Saskatchewan. I've waited for the school bus with six or seven brothers at a time so I have been in 127 fist fights, winning more than one-third. I have always wanted to be a rich cowboy and it has taken years to discover it is a contradiction in terms. I have been told I am a gifted storyteller and if you take one chapter in this book and read it over and over six or eight times it will be just like meeting me in person.

Occasionally I have been asked, "Are you a real cowboy?" My answer has always been the same. "I won't say I am, I won't say I'm not – but I will say that I'll do until a real cowboy shows up."

The stories I am about to tell you are true, as I remember them. The people in here that I have had the pleasure to know and tell you about really deserve a book each to themselves, real characters.

I'm also going to put in a couple stories that are complete bull for your enjoyment – see if you can pick them out.

Before I put pen to paper I said to my brother Blair, "This book will basically write itself – I already have the hard part done: the introduction and the ending!" He said, "You have the hard part done alright – you lived through it!"

There was an older gent in our hometown who was full of long-winded stories made up largely of names and dates. Most of his stories weren't terribly interesting; his chief claim to fame was he was the first baby born in Radisson, Saskatchewan. He caught my dad and me at the post office one day and said, "Albert, did I ever tell you the story about such and such?" My dad said, " Yes, Claude, many times." Claude never missed a beat and said, "Well it's a good story and bears telling again." I'll aspire to be a little more like him.

There was another old gent in town who was known for his tall tales of this and that, but one tale stands out. I was a young lad in the pool hall and this old fellow was telling of hunting partridges. For those of you who don't know these upland prairie game birds, partridges wait until the last moment, then all thunder away in a flock, startling and confusing their stalker.

This gent said he got his shotgun out and shot 11 in one shot – pretty amazing (and tallish, obviously).

My uncle said, "Eddie, why don't you just say you just shot an even dozen?" Eddie replied, "I'm not going to lie over one partridge!"

Well, I'm not going to lie over one partridge either. Here we go! My hope is that this book will be a best seller and maybe even a movie, and be on the back of toilets across the land – in some cases serving a dual purpose!

EARLY DAYS

First Memories

I grew up on a mixed farm in Saskatchewan. Our extended family lived in three houses. First, there was Great Gramma's house, the "Big House," and it was something: a living room, a parlor and two staircases, and running water; we would head over there for bath night and have to put on a skit or sing a song for the old folks before getting our bath. Then there was the little house in the same yard, where Grampa and Gramma lived. We ourselves lived in the house across the road.

I loved going over to Gramma's in the morning – she made the best breakfast. Then we would walk through the cow pasture and count the new calves.

Anyway, two short stories:

My older brother Greg and I would torment the rooster – he was a devil rooster and would chase the heck out of us. We would throw rocks at him and generally torment him. One day our neighbor kid come over and threw a stone and hit him in the head. We thought we'd killed him but we only knocked him out. So we took him to the garbage dump and covered him up. Well a couple days later he's back and he is pissed off.

He started chasing us and he was getting me, pecking and flapping. My brother came back and fought him off and I thought the rooster was killing him. Just then my gramma came flying out the house with a broom and saved the day.

My dad was in the barn witnessing all this and laughing his head off. Well after Grams got done with the rooster she went after Dad, whacking him with the broom for laughing.

Gramps showed up and the rooster took a run and jumped on him. As cool as a cucumber Gramps grabbed his feet and went to the chopping block with his axe. Chicken dinner.

I had a collie dog named Jiggs. We were inseparable. That dog went everywhere with me. One day he shows up and he is a mess. Quills everywhere. I was beside myself bawling. It was a bad deal. Gramps showed like he always did just at the right time. He took a potato fork (like a pitch fork only the tines are flat) and he stuck my dog's head to the ground, sat on him and expertly took all the quills out. I can honestly say that doing that procedure is not a spectator sport.

The Picture

This is very likely the thing that defines me the most. It is a picture that hung in my grandfather's office in Radisson. It's a cowboy jumping off his horse after roping a calf at a rodeo. I wanted to be that guy. Have a trained horse and saddle and the skill and talent to win a rodeo in calf roping. Being part of a family with so many kids and living far from town I didn't get to visit my grandfather's office that often, but when I did I never missed a chance to go look at that picture.

We finally had a colt born that I could call my own and I trained him to ride. But I didn't have a saddle. Indians rode bareback but to be a cowboy you needed a saddle. Our neighbors, the Brand boys, Harold and Bill, were great guys, the best at hockey and baseball – I remember my dad saying Harold Brand could shoot a puck through a barn door! They had a saddle but never used it. It was just hanging in their barn. I would ride over there and put it on my horse, no blanket, and ride home. Every once in a while they would come and retrieve it and then I would ride over and get it back again.

My grandfather Scott saw this scene play out many times and finally he said, "Here is $25 (a huge amount of money), go and buy that saddle." But he also gave me my first lesson in business. He said offer them $20; if they take it, you keep the five dollars, but don't lose the deal – if they want 25, pay it and you have the saddle. I made the deal – for $20. I rode that saddle for years, then all of my sons used it and it is hanging in my house right now. I hope that my sons' kids will use it. Some say I still have the five dollars.

Getting back to that picture in my grandfather's office, I have always had a passion for western art and have a modest collection of Doolittles and some others that have some monetary value but this picture has sentimental value, since it reminds me of my grandfather.

Time moved on and so did I and my grandfather passed on. They tore the old post office down and built a new one. No one really knew what became of all my grandfather's stuff but more than 30 years later I began searching for that picture. Wouldn't you know, my nephew Travis found it up north in a town called Prince Albert. I got it back and it looked just like I remembered it. It is now hanging in a special place in my house. It is exactly where it should be.

Three Short Stories

So growing up in rural Saskatchewan in the 50's and 60's the country was changing daily. The homesteading was over but just over. My granddad was a decorated World War One hero, an educated man who had the job of post master. I am four generations away from the true pioneers but my granddad was just one generation away. Our community at the time was a mix of German, Polish, Ukrainian, English and Scottish immigrants, men and women who were strong and tough and hard working – exactly what the country needed to be homesteaded. They were given a quarter section of land, they built on it, made improvements, and made it their home. It was a truly wonderful place to grow up in. My granddad would make sure that all these immigrants got all the benefits they were entitled to. My apology is this: these fine pioneers are only getting one short chapter each. Here they are.

Nick Bohankovich

I'll start with our neighbor down on the North Saskatchewan River. Nick Bohankovich was an old Russian. I don't know that I have the spelling right – but neither does anyone else. No one could pronounce his name so everyone called him Bone Cabbage. He had a quarter section full of stumps and stones and an old tractor with a four-foot disc. One tough way to make a living. Now at that time our farm was fourth generation, well-established with machinery and cattle. I would visit with Nick but it was more just to break the monotony of my job on the farm, which basically amounted to going round and round the field behind the plough. It was more just to get a look at Nick since I couldn't speak Russian and he couldn't speak English.

Just a footnote: I was seeding down there with a Massey 97 tractor with an 18-foot disker and a 15-foot disker hooked to it. That's a big outfit, that leaves a furrow behind you that you follow round and round till you are done. A little black jack rabbit got in the furrow and could not get out. He would run and run ahead of me but could not escape. He would give up and stop and then run again. He finally gave up and I had to pull the big hand clutch and stop. You didn't want to do this because it left a big unseeded patch in the field that you would get heck for later. I got off the tractor to let the little bugger out of the furrow and as a last act of desperation he bunted at me! I captured the little scrapper and carried him over to the fence line – you're on your own now, pardner!

Frank Stephanski

This story is really about two/three people. I'll just let it unfold.

I was about 28 when I met Frank, an old Polish bachelor. I moved back to the farm, one of my first loves, but wanted my own roof, so I bought a house in town from Alice and Wilmer Hamp, two of the nicest people on this earth, who I am friends with to this day. They sold me the old house and built a new one across the road from it and Frank Stephanski was on my other side.

I didn't have much of a lawn but I would mow it and when I did I would mow Frank's lawn also. He would invite me in his little home and pour us each a drink of straight whiskey. That was really a little too rough for me. Then he would show me letters and pictures from back home. It always intrigued me about how brave you have to be to strike out on your own to a new land like that. Frank had a crooked finger and he told me how he hid it from Immigration officials – just in case they wouldn't let in Polish immigrants with crooked fingers!

I will always remember – Frank's English wasn't that good – one time when I wanted to borrow a grass whip from Alice and Wilmer's garage, but it was locked. I asked Frank, "Do you know where the key is?" Frank replied, "Come mit me, Ernie, I show sometime place where key live."

Bert Shipovich

Bert was a good friend of my dad's and also a good friend of mine. He had a garage and also was the Massey Ferguson machinery dealer. It was also a real gathering place, almost like a coffee shop. Bert was always really busy.

My earliest memory was when I was a little guy in there with my dad and the men are all sitting around and I'm peeking out from the rows of parts. One of the men saw me and said, "What's your name, little boy?" I was shy and went back in the shelves of parts. I peeked out again and the same man, Bill Scott, says, "I know your name." and I'm thinking how's this ole guy know me? And he says, "Your name is Jim Turd." I guess I made a hell of a face and they all laughed, and that really pissed me off! I peeked out again and said, "I know your name," and that really got their attention, and I said, "sonofabitch!" Well, they all laughed and laughed, not what I was going for!

Anyway, back to Bert. Over my too-short farming career Bert would come to my rescue time and time again, cause I was good at breaking stuff and when I put a wrench in my hands I usually ended up hurting myself. It wasn't just me he was helpful to, though – Bert was like that to the whole farming community.

So I Lost My Marbles

When I was eight or 10 the neighbors down the road were moving away and having an auction sale. I remember being a little unsettled about it – why on earth would they want to leave? It was pretty exciting solely because it was out of the ordinary, with a big crowd, an auctioneer and hot dogs for sale. Well a big guy who looked about 16 or 18 came up to me. His name was Dale Assmus, and it was his family that was moving away. He asked me if I was interested in a treasure hunt. He had a map with so many steps from here and so many from there and an "x" marking the spot. This ranks right up there as one of the nicest things anyone ever did for me! So here we go – a real treasure hunt. He has a shovel and very likely embellished the situation a bit to add to the excitement, drama and thrills.

So we go out in the trees and follow the treasure map. We start digging but it didn't take long – the treasure was not very deep. What we dug up was three tobacco cans full of the nicest marbles you could imagine. They were beautiful. This was just like King Tut's tomb to me. I was on cloud nine.

I went home with my treasure and did the same thing. I drew a map and buried my treasure. I never saw those marbles again!

Now there are two schools of thought. One is: I have 10 brothers – how many eyes were watching me bury the marbles? So one of 'em coulda stole 'em.

Or I just simply lost them in the woods. They widened the road by the farm around that time and took away some of the bush. Maybe the marbles are in the road!

The Cattle Business

The cattle business is one of my first loves, one of. And it was something I took pride in thinking I was good at. My dad starting buying and fattening cattle of all types: bulls, cows, steers and heifers, anything that was bought cheap. Our cattle buyer, I loved this man, was a guy by the name of Bill Miller. He would say, "If they are bought right they're half sold." That's a big reason my dad was able to support 13 kids and keep us in skates, clothes and whatever else. Bill drank a quart of whiskey a day and could tell you what cattle you bought eight months ago.

Just a little note before we go on – I earned my first five dollars from Bill when I was about eight years old. He was out hunting partridges and lost his wrist watch. He got my dad to get all of us kids out to look for his watch around the bush he was hunting in. I was following right behind him cause I really liked him. Bill would keep sending me over a bit to look but I was soon just following him again. Wouldn't you know it – he stepped on his watch and picked it up unharmed. Bill gave me a five-dollar reward – and also a valuable lesson. He showed me how to fold the bill in half the long way, then again the short way and put it in your pocket like an arrow – so it wouldn't work its way or fall out. People who really know me ask me if I still have that same five dollars!

I remember my first meal in a restaurant. Can any of you say that? Well, first of all, living way out in the country, and second, this being in the mid-1950's, and third, coming from a family of 13, it isn't that unbelievable. This was back in the days of travel not being too prevalent and when you did travel you usually packed a lunch.

Dad was on his way to Saskatoon to the stockyards to discuss a cattle deal with his old friend (and later mine) and took me with him. This was right up my alley – I loved, and still do, everything about the cattle business. The auctioneers, the people, the action. They broke for lunch and there was a little cafeteria right in the same building. I sat with dad and the auctioneer and the cattle buyer – I felt like one lucky kid! I got to order a hamburger and french fries – two things really stick out – I'd had hamburger of course lots of times at home but never french fries and never hamburger bun.

So I loaded 'er up with lots of ketchup and there was a big drop of ketchup about to drip down the bottle so I did what any kid would do – I licked that drip off. That kinda stopped the conversation for a moment, then they all laughed.

I did not want this kind of attention and then Dad said, "Son – we don't lick the ketchup bottle when we're away from home." I live by that rule to this day.

So Dad started a feed lot, but without the lot part. We had the worst facilities – no, that's not right, we had *no* facilities. I remedied that later by building great corrals with water bowls and wind fences and swinging gates – I love that kind of work.

When we got rolling the cattle truck, a three-ton Dodge with the old "Hartford Insurance" sign on the side, would go to Saskatoon once a week, hauling in a load of fat cattle for butcher and taking back a load of tail-enders – anything that was cheap. My dad was a farmer and a good one. He grew lots of barley and had lots of sons so this system worked pretty darn well. We would brand, dehorn 'em and anything else and then fatten 'em up and take 'em to town. That's how most of us got university educations.

Around this time, I branched out a bit myself. I bought three herds of cattle in July – cows with calves at foot, six or eight from Don Konchuck, six or eight from Adolf Kaul and about the same from Oleg Gust, all for $650 a pair. Well that January I sold all the calves for about $650 each – I had a herd of cows lookin at me that were free and clear. Try and tell me something about the cattle business – I already knew it all!

So later that spring, about April, another herd come up for sale – 30 cows, some with calves, some not calved out yet – for $700 each. Well, I went to make the deal and the fellow said, "No, the price now is $750." That was my chance to get out but I didn't. I bought 'em and some of those cattle didn't calve till late in the fall so I didn't have much to sell back – and the cattle prices were dropping. I lost my behind on that deal. I also started figuring maybe I didn't quite know everything about the cattle business.

Now I'm fourth generation on this same farm. My great granddad, my granddad, my dad all made a living even through the "dirty thirties" on the same ground – we have a hundred-year plaque that the government awards for that achievement, that they gave my dad in 2001. So when it came to the cattle business I had some clout. In those days you would go to town, buy some cattle or a swather or whatever, and go to the back and duke it out with the Canadian Imperial Bank of Commerce manager, a guy by the name of Vern Wittman. Vern was old style. Had his sleeves rolled up and wore a tie most days. Every once in a while he'd get drunk at the bar and get in a fist fight. You couldn't ask for a better man.

I'd just got married and rented a place north of town. It had water bowls and good corrals – calves had peaked over a dollar a pound the year before and just then had fallen back to the 70 cent mark. Harvest was over and I had a good crop in the bin. So I went into town and told my cattle buyer and good friend – you guessed it, Bill Miller – to start buyin' up those cheap cattle. Well, I forgot to tell him to stop and I wound up with 140 calves – I was in over my head! There was also another catch. Remember I said the cattle business was "*one* of my first loves?" Well, my first love was horses. You cannot be a cowboy without one.

In 1982 I went to the classiest horse sale I've ever seen and bought a fancy world class yearling stallion for $7100 (maybe more on this later). At that time a good using horse was anywhere from $800 all the way up to $1500. But I trusted in myself on this and in the end it worked out.

But now I gotta' put the bell on the cat. I mustered up all the strength I had and went in to see Vern the banker. My plan was to put the horse invoice in the middle of all the cattle invoices and slip it by Vern. Well, turns out bankers are trained and paid for looking after little details. Vern absolutely blew a gasket, I never saw him so mad, and he hadn't got to the horse yet! So he said I'm not cashing this check (the horse). He finally got calm and we worked out a plan. Bill Miller sat on his invoices for a week and I started hauling canola to Lloydminster and covered close to half the debt. At this time I gotta' say it was great men like my forefathers and neighbors that settled and built this great country but they couldn't have done it without great chance-taking bankers like Vern. I remember my dad coming home with our first manure spreader. Now that made our job a lot easier. Before this we would fork the manure from the barn on a stone boat and then fork it off by hand out in the field. I was pretty excited and said to Dad, "Is that your manure spreader?" Dad said, "Yep, mine and the banker's!" I walked away thinking, "What the hell does the banker want with a manure spreader?" By the way, don't put any big rocks in 'em. A very few of you will know what I mean!

I'd like to put in a little history here about our family cattle brand. Branding is a very necessary form of identification that really hasn't needed any improvement since inception – it still works just fine, though I can see the tree-huggers out there rolling their eyes.

My great grandfather Albert Longely Nutting registered this brand in Regina, Northwest Territories in the fall of 1902 – three years before Saskatchewan and Alberta became provinces. Albert Longely passed it on to Chester Albert (my granddad), who passed it down to James Albert (my dad), then to me, James Ernest, and then I passed it down to my eldest son, James Carson, the current owner. The publication of this book will coincide with the 115th year of the continuous use of the same cattle brand under the Nutting name! If you know of an older brand that stayed in the same family surname, on either side of the 49th parallel, please let me know – there will be damn few, if any at all. I have the original branding irons hanging in my house. I also have the original registration papers – one for the horse brand and location (left hip), the same for the cattle brand. I also have the original copy of the Canadian Brand Act, framed with barn wood from our Saskatchewan homestead hanging in my home. I have a one-year-old grandson, Levi James Nutting, who, when the time comes, I hope will register and use that brand on cattle of his own.

My Ear Operation

Before any of us became what we became we had to grow up, learn, evolve, etc. One brother became a very successful heart surgeon but before that he was just a farm kid hanging out with his buddies drinking beer and throwing the bottles at signs.

When he was going to medical school in Saskatoon I was rooming with him and was a high dollar Pen Rider in a cattle feed lot – in other words, we were basically starving. One of his student doctor buddies (who is now a famous plastic surgeon, we will call him Doctor Wayne) and my brother and I were out drinking in a tavern near the university and I was complaining that I had lumps in my earlobes and that they were very itchy. Dr. Wayne said, "What a coincidence, we just took that in class today. What you do is cut them out, send the growths to the lab to see if they are coniferous or deciduous (OK – I made that part up) and then sew the lobe back up."

So we did that.

We snuck into the operating room in the university hospital at 9:00 pm, did the minor surgery and were back drinking beer within the hour. But I gotta tell ya – I have tied up grain sacks neater than this guy tied up my ear lobes. He did the right thing and sent the lumps to the lab to see if they were malignant or benign. I have scars in my earlobes to this day. To tell you the truth it really didn't bother me much – gives ya character plus makes for a good story.

The funny part is I didn't see Dr. Wayne for a few weeks and when I did he had this sheepish look on him. We were back in the same tavern and he admitted, "The next day after your operation I read a little farther – you're supposed to cut the lumps out from the back of the ear – then you don't see a scar at all!"

There is a moral in there somewhere, maybe more than one. Good idea at the time? Get what you pay for?? I'll leave a space below and you can add yours.

My Life of Crime

So I entered a life of crime. Around 1978 our good school board officials decided to tear down our beautiful four-story brick school building and put up a shiny new tin shed. Can you believe it? Well, the powers that be took out what they wanted – desks, fixtures, slate blackboards, etc. – and then in came the wrecking ball. A tragedy, really.

My uncle Alex, a real character, always full of mischief and with a knack for getting under people's skin (cut away – he snuck two 7's out of the card deck that the old guys played crib with – they played all winter before discovering this) went in and literally rescued the big beautiful school bell from the wreckage. The powers that be said they were going to build a brick cairn and put the bell in it, and sent the police out to get it. They did and it really left a bone in my uncle's throat. My friend Kenny and I were in the Shadow Room of the Radisson Hotel drinking beer with Uncle Alex and he was still sore about having to give the bell back.

A plan started to form then and there. I said, "Kenny, let's steal the bell back!" I knew it was sitting in the furnace room in the school. I also knew from past experience how to get in.

When we were back in school we would go to the boys' room, push the window open, crawl outside, push the window closed and have a smoke. When we were done we took a nail, pried the window back open and crawled back inside. The teachers never caught us.

I said, "Come on, Kenny, let's go." He was not a real willing accomplice. Kenny was way too nervous for crime. He said, "Let's plan this out," I said, "It's planned, all you have to do is let me out and keep driving around the block."

I got in the bathroom window, found the bell in the furnace room, and made my escape through the front doors. Boy that bell was heavy. Kenny came driving around the corner and I was under the street light with my foot on the bell and had my thumb out. Kenny damned near had a heart attack.

We drove out to our farm and hid the bell in the barn hay loft, which was full of hay bales, and were back in the Radisson Hotel within the hour. We let Alex in on our caper and I know he went to his grave years later a happy man. This kind of deal was right up his alley.

Back to Kenny. He was a good mechanic – he worked in Froom's Garage on Main Street and was a really handy hockey player – but he was no criminal.

He phoned me and said, "They might be on to us – the cops drove by the shop five times today." Well, Ken – you are *on* Main Street!

They did not discover the bell was missing until they built the brick cairn and were having a ceremony with various dignitaries. They go to get the bell – it's not there – awkward! There were very few people who saw any humor in this, in fact they were really mad. Reward out, threats made, etc.

Now it's a mystery and Alex was having a ball. He would start a new rumor every week on where the bell was. Years later I am on a skiing charter holiday in Lake Tahoe. As usual on these trips you meet really interesting people. I teamed up with a guy from Thunder Bay, Ontario and asked two girls out for dinner. We are getting acquainted and he says he's from Thunder Bay, the girls say they are from Regina and I say I'm from Saskatoon. The girls come clean and say they are really from Ituna, a little town near Regina. So I come clean and say, "Well, I was just acting big, I'm really not from Saskatoon I'm really from Radisson." One of the girls says, "Radisson, Radisson, what do I know about Radisson? Was there a school bell stolen there?" I damned near fell on the floor. We are in a casino restaurant in Lake Tahoe, California, more than a thousand miles from home, and the connection was there right in front of us. Uncle Alex's son, Mick, my cousin, married a beautiful girl from Ituna and that's how the story made it to Lake Tahoe.

Just to wrap up the school bell mystery. Years later I was back in the Shadow Room with two local guys having a beer. One of the guys was Kenny's brother. I said, come on guys and we drove out to the Hopewell school yard where I had s tashed the bell after relocating it from the hayloft after my two younger brothers had discovered it, much to their astonishment. We picked it up and I placed it in the cairn. I went back to Radisson for its 100-year anniversary. I wandered over to where the school bell was bolted and held in place with steel rods to keep it in place in the brick cairn. I couldn't help but notice what thickness the rods were and what size wrench you'd need for those bolts.

There are three casinos (or were back then) in Lake Tahoe. Dolly Parton was performing in one, Frank Sinatra in another and in the third was women's mud wrestling. You guessed it, I've always been a patron of the arts, so we headed to the mud wrestling. They had beautiful well-endowed girls in the mud ring wearing bathing suits. I ask you, what is not to like. The announcer asked if anyone was "brave" enough to go in the ring with them. You change out of your clothes and they give you overalls and in you go. Now, I am a young healthy farm boy and I am gonna feel the hell out of those girls, so – "Hold my coat!" What a surprise! I got dumped so hard on my head and held under mud till I was gasping for breath and just when I was gonna cop a feel they would slam me again. I finally surrendered and got all cleaned up and the four of us head out for dinner. We go to Harrah's and get seated. I get up to go to the bathroom and walk by a backroom. There is a party going on and guess who is in there: Frank Sinatra.

By now you know I am far from being shy. I go right up and introduce myself to Frank and tell him my situation: I'm with these new friends and it would be "big medicine" to me if you could walk up and say, "Ernie, what are you doing in Tahoe? Why didn't you tell me? I'll get you tickets!" Something like that. He said let me see what I can do and I left it like that.

I went back and joined my party and did not say a word. Ordered and chatted and finally the meal came. But so did a lot of commotion. Big as you please up walks Frank Sinatra. True to script he says, "Ernie – what a surprise – how long are you here for?"

I say, "Gee, Frank, not now, can't you see I'm eating?"

Lost in Translation

This is a little story about skiing. My brother Stew and I have gone skiing on a good portion of the ski hills in the West. It's a great sport and you meet great people along the way. This particular story is about meeting and skiing with these two guys from Japan. We shared the same quad chair going up the mountain and struck up a conversation of sorts. The one guy could speak a little English and the other fellow none at all. But we got by and spent the day skiing together. Then we got back to the lodge and got some grub and a beer.

Now I gotta switch gears. At that time I had just got out of Lakeland College in Vermilion, Alberta. My brother was going to university on his way to becoming a pretty darn famous heart surgeon. My aspirations lay elsewhere. I wanted to be a cowboy and a cattleman. I was taking a course in animal husbandry, primarily raising livestock. Part of the course was in artificial insemination. The hardest part of the course was spelling it.

So back at the ski lodge. We're having a beer with these Japanese guys and

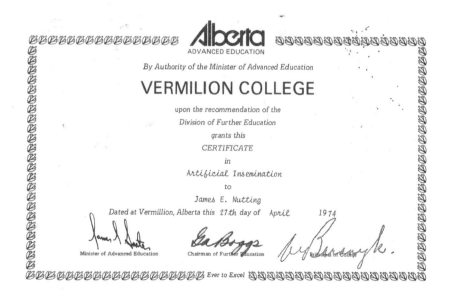

trying to explain what we do. The first guy makes a hammering motion and then puts his thumb in his mouth – he's a carpenter. My brother makes the motion of putting a stethoscope to his ears and listening to someone's heart. Doctor! Now me! But how the heck do you convey the idea of impregnating livestock? I'm quite sure we didn't get the message across because the Japanese guy just kept laughing and shaking his head and saying, "No, no, no!"

Several more tries at it didn't make it any clearer. All I can say is that that Japanese feller kind of kept his distance after that.

Just a footnote on skiing. I prided myself on being quite a good skier, and as my four boys came along I was fortunate enough to have the time and money to take them skiing with me. I was going to teach them how to be fast and stylish – and I would have, too, if I could have ever caught up with them!

Coincidence Man

I don't really know how to begin this story. I was still back on the farm and in the summer Mom and Dad would take the younger kids up north in Saskatchewan to Waskesiu Lake, where they rented cabins. There was the lake and a beautiful golf course, just a great all-round getaway.

But us bigger kids never got to go – that was haying season, meaning we stayed home and cut and baled hay and hauled it to the back yard. This particular year we got the haying all done and my brothers Lawrence, Tony and I headed up there with our golf clubs and a tent for a weekend. We were by no means experienced campers but we picked out a site with a picnic table and fire pit, pitched the tent, cooked supper and went to bed. I was awakened by some noise and got out of the tent to witness what was left of our grub with a small black bear just finishing cleaning up on all our groceries, ending with licking out the butter container. I chased him off and went back to bed. The next morning we are at the little store picking up more supplies. I told the grocery guy of our plight with the bear cleaning us out and he said, "Well, you learned a valuable lesson there."

"OK, what was the lesson we learned?"

He said, "You learned not to keep your food in your tent – the bear will come inside to get it." The truth is we never thought of that, but that was exactly what we had planned to do!"

The rest of the weekend came and went somewhat uneventfully with golfing, camping, etc., and just when we were packing up a young park ranger shows up and is asking all kinds of questions, kinda out of the blue. It was really a little annoying. He was checking out our gear and vehicle – oddball stuff. "Where's your axe?" The fact of the matter was that we forgot to bring one and borrowed an axe from our neighboring camper to split firewood.

We left for home and he followed us out to the park boundary. Two weeks later harvest is in full swing and I came in the house for dinner and my dad answers the phone and says there is a park ranger who wants to talk with you.

"Are you Ernie Nutting?"

"Yes I am."

"Do you drive a 73 Dodge Duster licence such and such?"

"Yes I do."

"I want you to prepare to face charges for cutting down a tree in a national park."

"I didn't cut down a tree in a national park."

"Yes you did, we have witnesses who saw you."

"Well now, you got me if you have witnesses that saw me do it, but wait a minute – I didn't cut down a tree, there is no possible way you can have witnesses – you must be lying. I didn't cut down a tree, you can't have witnesses, you are a liar and don't call here again." Click.

Now from past experiences my dad knew these angelic sons of his got into trouble from time to time, but this time was different – we were innocent!

Now for the co-incidence. At the same time we were up camping there were also three young guys camping and golfing. For argument's sake I'm gonna call them Kelly Hall, Dean Radcliffe and Sheldon Le Lievre. The real story is this. They were golfing in a light rain and a golf club slipped out of their hands and stayed up in a spruce tree. They threw a few more clubs up to knock it out of there and two more clubs stayed lodged in the tree. They came back just before nightfall with a box of beer and some lawn chairs – and chopped the tree down and rescued the clubs!

The park ranger suspected them of chopping down the tree and they said, "No, we are too law-abiding of citizens to pull a dastardly prank like that – it was probably those farm boys over at the campground!"

We found out later that the park ranger even came back and told Kelly, Sheldon and Dean, "You guys are off the hook, we found the real culprits." Turns out that these three guys were going to the University of Saskatchewan with my brothers. They hooked up somewhere somehow and became friends. It was only a few weeks after this incident they came out to the farm and were relating their side of this golf-club tree-cutting incident. Can you imagine the look on our faces!

We are still friends with these gangsters to this day, and of course when we get together this story always comes out and just like us the story gets better with age!

Not About Family

This book is supposed to be about life's experiences – mostly uplifting ones. My apologies for this – it can't be all about family and friends because there are simply way, way too many omissions. If you are not mentioned in this book – call me. You will be in the next one! Promise!

Now I gotta tell ya about my brother Robert. He is not with us anymore but touched deeply everyone who knew him – and they all have their own favorite story. If he only had put pen to paper he would have written a best seller.

I firmly believe Bob was a true genius. He simply could not sit through formal education because it was way too slow and boring. So he turned his energies to more creative things – pranks, shenanigans and stirring the pot, uprisings – getting the picture?

The teacher awarded Bob with a grade 8 certificate provided he would never walk through their school door again. So at the tender age of 16 he found himself working for Texas Instruments in Egypt. Coincidentally, right at the same time Anwar Sadat got assassinated. There is no evidence this involved Bob but it sure as hell affected him! The country was in uproar, martial law was invoked, foreigners were detained, some taken for ransom, etc. The company Bob worked for said leave, go now, escape – which they did! They drove their Land Cruiser across the Sinai desert (the battlefield of the six-day war between Egypt and Israel) on the way to Israel.

They had a cargo of dynamite, as they were doing seismic work. The trick was that having dynamite was now cause for being labeled a terrorist. So the solution they came up with was this. They stuffed all the dynamite in a disabled tank that was abandoned in the desert from the war with the intention of blowing all the dynamite and the tank to smithereens. Which they did. There were some minor complications. The blasting wire did not work so they lit 'er up with toilet paper. Then they got behind a sand dune and their Jeep. That covered the sideways blast. Then big chunks of metal started falling from the sky! My brother and his partner crawled under the Jeep and the two other guys got in it and drove it away.

They all survived that one and I have some pretty nifty "Before and After" photos.

To call Bob the "black sheep" would be very understated to say the least. He had a great moral compass, for which I give credit to our parents and all our forefathers. It was simply the general rules and guidelines didn't seem to suit him.

Case in point. There was a time I got on an airplane in Saskatoon flying to see another brother in Toronto and here is Bob sitting on the plane. I hadn't seen him in at least a year, so I said, "Come sit with me – there's an empty seat." He couldn't comply – he was handcuffed to a sheriff! I believe it was over bringing diamonds in the country without going through customs. He'd had a briefcase (I remember it vividly) with a false bottom. On one occasion when he came home from overseas he showed me about 30 diamonds, the size of my little fingernail, in a purple velvet cloth inside a purple velvet pouch! They were enchanting!

Another Ski Trip

My brothers and I would get together every New Years and go skiing. For six or seven years our destination was Whitefish, Montana – and I would recommend that destination to anyone. One year Bob couldn't make it and offered to meet us in Italy as an alternative. My brother Lawrence was going to university at the time and I was working on the farm with my dad. I should take a moment to clarify that. Dad worked and Mom never took a job. She just hung around the house cooking and cleaning and baking for 13 kids in the days of wringer washers and clotheslines, winter and summer. More about this later.

Back to the ski trip. Bob said, "Come to Italy – I will arrange everything." Talk about famous last words! I said to mom, we can't go, it's out of the question for so many reasons. Number 1 we can't afford it!

Her reply was wonderful. Affording it is the last of your worries – you firstly need your health, then you need the time, and lastly you need finances. She would be so proud of her kids now, having instilled such a "can do" pioneering spirit.

So we bought two tickets to London, England in 1981 – and never heard another word from Bob.

Back to the ski trip. We never heard a word from Bob. Remember I mentioned the president of Egypt getting assassinated. Well, it left the country in chaos! Bob and his crew were running for their lives! Dad had written our whole itinerary on the back of an envelope: "The train to Rome leaves Victoria station every day at noon." That was it! So off we went – and what an adventure. I'll start with the nine hour flight. There were several of us that wanted to get the party started. The stewardesses – bless their hearts – served everyone a drink, then retired. My brother Lawrence found where the booze was kept and we drank it all! Partied the whole flight. As they were preparing to land the stewardesses showed up again and one girl said to me, "Sir, we are short 30 bottles (the airplane ones) of champagne." I wonder why she was asking me?

Now – Heathrow Airport. We had to get help to get outta there. A kind police woman gave us help. She told us directions and to queue for a taxi – we found out soon enough queue means line up. We got a "bed and breakfast" which we never used and headed out to see what London had to offer. This was back in the day when pubs were getting bombed by Irish terrorists, and some had signs "Soldiers not served here."

We somehow split up and Lawrence spent the night in a fancy hotel on the Thames River and I spent the night running from druggies!

We hooked up again in the morning and got on the train at Victoria station. The train went to Dover on the coast and then it went in the belly of a ship and across the English Channel and docked at Calais, France.

Then back on the train. The train was pretty darn full and I got up and wandered around a bit and found an empty car. I went back and got my brother and was just about to have the first sleep of my trip when this big railroad porter hit my feet with his stick and sent us back to the "cattle car." Apparently we were in first class!

There was still no word from Bob and we changed plans – if we had stuck to the plan he would have been on the platform in Rome waiting for us. We explained our plight to two Americans we met, and they gave us two words of advice: 1) Do not take the subway in Paris as the train drops you off at the north of Paris and starts again at the south of Paris. Take a taxi; and 2) There is great skiing in a little town called Bardonecchia – jump off there.

So that's what we did. We got through Paris – they are rude and the whole damn works of 'em speak English – but not to you – and headed on our journey. We got to Bardonecchia at about 3:30 in the morning, dark as hell and cold too. I jumped off the train and four soldiers or police officers started going nuts in Italian, talking fast and loud and pointing. I stepped back on the train and they quit. I stepped off again and they went into their act. I stepped on again and they quit. I said, "Hey Lawrence, you gotta see this." So I did it again – same thing. Lawrence said the train station is on this side.

Anyhow, here we are. The train station was open – no doors – I remember watching Lawrence sleeping on a marble slab while I was keeping watch on all our gear. Way too much gear – we even brought our own skis and boots – that one is on the learning curve. I was thinking we gotta get a hotel room and get some sleep, all we've been doing is drinking and traveling, if we don't get something to eat and sleep we're gonna be sick!

Finally, a gal shows up and gets behind the wicket. I go over there and ask about a hotel, and I really don't know if she was having fun with me or not but there was no response. But I had an ace in the hole. My lovely (and practical) soon-to-be sister-in-law had given me an Italian/English translation book so I got it out and began to slaughter the Italian language. The girl soon found her English skills and directed us to an "umbergo".

A little corner store was open and there was a picture of a milkshake "Frappe" and there were bags of something that turned out to be potato chips – that was our first Italian meal: potato chips and a milkshake. We got a hotel room, not quite what we expected, there was a bit of a snow drift on the inside of the balcony door. The toilet was a porcelain pad with a hole in the middle and a cord you pulled to "flush." I said to myself – I'm not using that! Well you do!

The next day we headed out skiing. We hooked up with two British commandos on leave and had a ball. That night we explored all the bars and met up with an Italian bartender who wanted to ski with us the next day. We decided to do a little "off roading" and accidentally skied down the wrong side of the mountain, leaving us a good five or six miles from town. We came across a park warden outpost and he agreed to tow us to town. Aggravating the problem, our tow rope was only six feet long. So one guy would hold the rope and put his ski poles back to the next guy and so on. Took forever to get back to town. The town was right out of a children's storybook, shop after shop after shop, butcher, baker, candlestick maker, and every one of 'em sold wine. If you wanted to go elsewhere they would take your bottle and put it back on the shelf for you to finish the next day. There was the odd glitch with the language barrier. One day on the slope I was reading a sign that was in French, German and Italian when someone hit me on the back of the head HARD! Now I don't care what the sign said or what rule I was breaking, I was not gonna put up with this kind of treatment. I turned around to fight – whoever hit me was in for it! I was just in time to avoid getting hit in the back with another "poma lift." The sign said, "Don't stand here or you will get hit on the head with the ski lift."

We finally got word from Bob. He waited for us in Rome for two days then went to England to our relatives and would be there to spend Christmas together. This time we did meet up and had a wonderful Christmas experience in Bolham Manor in Retford, northern England.

Every day was another experience. The only traffic accident we saw was one that we were in – Bob driving one car and me the other. Finally, it was time to head back to the colonies. I'm certain our English hosts had mixed feelings: tremendous relief and exhilaration!

Now for the trip home. We get on the train and I'm a little sick and need to use the bathroom. Bob says you can't use the bathroom when we're at the station. I asked why and he replied, "I don't know," so I went anyway. I sat on the toilet and looked out at the platform – and the people on the platform could look at me – that's why! Soooo I tried to pretend I was sitting on a regular seat instead of a toilet .

There was a tooth brush by the sink and I thought that's a good idea as I had a bad case of "hangover mouth." Just as I started brushing my teeth this guy comes in and says, "What the hell do you think you're doing – that's my toothbrush!" I said, "Gee Sir, I'm so sorry – I thought it was the railroad's!"

OK – I made that last part up! Pretty damn funny, though!

We get to Heathrow and the plane we are to take home is still froze up in Edmonton, Canada. We have twelve hours to kill in the Heathrow Airport. We spend our time drinking duty free whiskey and playing cards with "ex pats," a term Bob gave us meaning ex-patriots, people who make a living working out of their own country. We finally board the plane home pickled as can be – they would never let you board a plane in that kind of shape in this day and age! What a great adventure!

Now the strangest thing happened. All three of us got married very shortly after our trip, with Bob being the hold out. He came back again from overseas to be my best man, but he was in a body cast! He claimed he was hang gliding in the desert and had had an accident! So we will go with that. I had a sneaking suspicion it had more to do with diamonds and poor choice of company! The closer we got to the big day the more Bob would whittle away at his cast, kind of a "Doctor, heal thyself" type of thing. He said he just took cast material off the places it didn't hurt. By the time of the wedding he just had plaster on his one ankle and foot.

Then something else happened. Something wonderful. Bob discovered someone that was always there and she discovered something in Bob that was always there: Bob was leading a life on the edge. Don't take these words lightly – it was not sustainable. I truly believe that his bride literally saved his life. They went on to carve out a life together that brought happiness to themselves and everyone else – and you know it wouldn't have been easy. First one kid, then another, then another. They moved up north and bought a small ranch and went to work. This changed everything – even his name – Bob went from Bob to Robert.

Our whole family would head up to their place every year to enjoy their wonderful hospitality. Robert had a speed boat, "Northern Pleasure," and a pontoon boat and we would fish and swim and waterski and barbeque. We made memories up there that all the aunts and uncles and nieces and nephews will cherish forever. To this day the nieces and nephews are best friends because of the hospitality of Robert and Gail. The experiences and adventures we all had up there could fill a book itself.

My sons and I got to enjoy their company even more as we would go up there for their 4-H calf show and also every fall would head up to Pierceland to hunt. There were a few reasons for this. One is that the deer hunting is second to none and maybe more importantly our lodging and grub were second to none. Brother Robert and his family treated me and the boys like kings. Huge early morning breakfasts and great suppers. I remember thinking, I gotta pick my game up, cooking-wise, so I tried to make spaghetti and meat sauce like Uncle Robert and one of my boys commented, "I wonder what Uncle Robert puts in his?"

We also got to watch the animated movie "Spirit" every night as his youngest daughter had him on the "12 step" going to bed program. You know: movie, water, popcorn, bathroom, story, etc. I know that my sons, when it's time for them to look back and reflect, will remember these times as the very best times of their lives!

Then tragedy struck – twice. In two separate instances barely six months apart Gail and her daughters lost the only two men in their lives. I have no idea where you get the strength to go through something like this. Having lost someone close at a tender age, I know the pain but a mother having to go thru the loss of a young child has to be infinitely worse. Seeing that small northern community come together was simply amazing. Words cannot describe it. I do not know how they got through that but Gail still had a big job to do and boy did she ever step up to the plate. She and her absolutely beautiful precious daughters are doing fine. This story is far, far from over.

Elvis Pooyak

This is without a doubt the funniest story I know. It's about my old friend Ken. My circle of friends and acquaintances was pretty small when I was back on the farm. We just didn't get out much – this is not a complaint, more an observance. I made it to every rodeo I could as a spectator but I really wanted to be a contestant. Ken was a rodeo cowboy and it was back in the day when you entered every event. Not that that's rare, it's just that most cowboy athletes focus on what they're best at. Just by coincidence a guy I hadn't met yet was a contractor and his bull "Jim Bean" pretty much ended Ken's career. In those days hardly anyone made a living rodeoing – the money just wasn't there. Ken also worked at being a salesman at Hunter's Trailer and Marine, the biggest boat and motor home retailer in Canada. I went in there one time to buy a boat and told the owner I could get that boat cheaper somewhere else (a lie). The owner, Harry, said, "No you can't, son, I bought every boat the manufacturer made."

I was in there visiting with Ken and I said, "You know, Ken, you're likely the best cowboy I know." In true fashion to his character he said, "Well, no I'm not, my neighbor Elvis is a better cowboy." Now I've never met Elvis. Still ain't. I said who's Elvis? Ken replied he's a community pasture rider, Elvis Pooyak and he's one hell of a hand. That's as close as cowboys get to a compliment. That name struck me as being really unique and stayed with me for a long time. Many years later I'd moved out of the north and bought a small ranch in the foothills of Alberta. One of my very first purchases was two black ponies, a gelding and a mare – we named them Velvet and Elvis Pooyak.

The kids had a ball with them and we trained them to pull a wagon and sleigh also. I gave Elvis the pony to my eldest son, Carson.

Now let's slide ahead 15 years. Carson is a student at the University of Saskatchewan and he is at the lounge having a beer. He is wearing an Austin's Saddlery hat and the waitress said, "Do you know Austin?" My son says yes, he's one of my Dad's best friends. The gal says, "He's one of my dad's best friends too!" "What's your dad's name?" "Elvis Pooyak."

Can you imagine my son's expression – who would name someone after his pony? Well, that math didn't work!

I lost track of Ken for many years. Then we bumped into each other at a rodeo, of all places. We keep in touch through social media. I hope Ken writes a book – I've also said he would make one hell of a leader of the whole country!

Austin

I don't know where to put this chapter in the book. I have admired the way this next guy has conducted himself since I can remember. In 1976 he was the Novice Saddle Bronc Champ of Canada. He walked away from what would have been a heck of a successful rodeo life to become one of the best saddle makers in the business. I should know – I've got one of 'em sitting in my living room right now.

Austin and his brother Jay have run a successful fair-and-square western store forever. I used to go to North Battleford quite frequently, and when I did I'd stop in at Austin's place whenever I could. He had everything in there I needed. I moved up to Buffalo Narrows and would stop back first with one boy, then two, then three, then four. Austin used to joke, "You sure you got all them kids?"

When my oldest son was about six years old he said to Austin, "My dad says if you don't got it, we don't need it." That made Austin smile.

I will wager that I may be one of the last guys to trade colts for store merchandise. I once hauled eight colts back from Radisson to my ranch in Caroline and I stopped in to visit Austin. I said I got homes for four of 'em. Austin said unload 'em and let me take a look. I tied the colts up alongside the trailer and Austin said I'll take the other four. We decided on a price and then I said, "You know, money doesn't have to change hands here – I do all my shoppin' in your store anyway." So me and the boys got hats, boots, jeans and shirts and tack till we were square again.

Getting Lucky

This is a story about the luckiest night of my life. I was out in Radisson to take my crop off. I got rained out so I went into Battleford to see Austin. I told him I wanted to buy a great big ol' car to haul kids to hockey games (I had four boys in minor hockey – I know I passed myself on the road a few times).

Austin told a cowboy buddy of his that sold cars – a team roper named Louis (actually he wasn't that good of a team roper – he just had stumps for thumbs). I bought the nicest car I've ever owned: a used 1989 white Lincoln town car. What a beauty. They had a draw for $500 every month at the dealership and Louis said we better take a pic of you – you look lucky. Well of course the fix was in.

The dealership bragged that people drove 600 miles to deal there. I told them if I won the draw to give the check to Austin and I would get it when I saw him. They did.

I was really happy with my new purchase and wanted to drink a bottle of whiskey. Austin couldn't join me yet because he was still working. So I headed off to the Indian casino and proceeded to win just shy of 2000 bucks. Austin finally showed up and we did get a lot of that whiskey in us.

The next morning, I wake up looking at a strange ceiling in an unfamiliar room. I smell coffee and I'm as interested as anyone to find out where the hell I am. Well, Austin had driven me home to his place and it was a beautiful Saskatchewan fall morning. I am as fuzzy as can be and we head out to the deck to have coffee. Now my pockets are full of crumpled up $100 bills and I see this shiny white Lincoln car and I say, "Austin, that car is a beauty!" He said, "You bought that yesterday!" I was happy all over again!

Oh, I gotta slip in another bear story. This may be the funniest one I've heard. Austin's boy Troy told me this and I know I won't do it the justice that he does. They were camping in North Saskatchewan and woke up to a small black bear sitting on the picnic table with a gallon can of beans under one arm and a big bag of potato chips under the other. Just living the dream. Austin picked up a switch and walked up to him and wacked that little bear right between the eyes. Troy said, "That bear dropped everything and the look in his eye said IT'S ON." He chased Austin around the truck – then remembered himself and started getting the heck out of there, this time with Austin chasing him. That would have been good watching.

Let's get back to the saddle. The saddle I bought off Austin is a work of art. It has buffalos stamped on it and was my present to me for running a pretty tough fuel business up in Buffalo Narrows for eight years. I rodeod in that saddle, towed my buddy across a river in it, packed an elk my son shot down a mountain in it and on and on, and it was in rough shape. Unbeknownst to me, my son took it back to Austin, who revamped it, fixed the saddle horn, made a really neat breast plate, added a set of angora goat saddle bags, and made matching tapaderos stirrups. Then he flew down to Fort Worth, Texas to deliver it to me. It is my favorite possession.

We cruised around Texas for a week. I took him to Roy Cooper's Ranch, Billy Minnick's bar "Billy Bob's," and all the great sights and sounds of Texas.

Hank III was playing in a small venue in the stockyard in Fort Worth and was sold out. I said to the door guys, "My friend is all the way down from Canada – any way you could let us in? The doorman said, "Yep, in ya go." Boy I love Texas. If you know Hank III, half his stuff is really rough country and then he has some heavy metal. The crowd reflected this in that half of 'em were wearing cowboy lids and the other half looked like they'd had a really bad day of fishing. Hooks and bolts and pins in their lips and cheeks and eyebrows. One such guy walked by Austin and me and said, "You guys want a beer?" Austin looked at me and I said "Sure." We don't do that in Canada – besides, beer is $1.50 in Texas. Boy, I love Texas.

The Bank Robbery

I was in my early 20's and was a surveyors' helper on the TransCanada Pipeline living in Kenora, Ontario. Kenora is situated by the Lake of the Woods – hundreds of lakes and islands in beautiful Northern Ontario. I was living the dream. My pay went up from $300 a month as a pen rider in a cattle feed lot in Saskatoon to making $500 a week for work that was not hard at all. The beauty of this was we were kept busy enough plus it was all out of town so you couldn't spend your money. It simply had to stack up!

I got into town early enough one night that I got to do a little shopping. I bought a beautiful suede denim jacket and headed off to the bar. The night was full of drinking and dancing but none of my buddies were around. The darned waitresses over-served me and I sat down but noticed my brand new jacket was gone! Don't that take all – someone stole my coat! I was fuming mad! I couldn't get the waitresses' attention so I drank up the drinks on the table. Then I spotted a jacket just like mine three or four tables down. Well, fair is fair, I looked around, grabbed that jacket and headed back to my seat. The band stopped around then and a bunch of strangers started sitting down at my table. "Who are you, who drank our drinks?" they said. It almost turned into a donnybrook but I argued a bit and finally left and went home.

I pieced 'er all together the next day – you didn't need to be Sherlock Holmes. I simply got drunk, sat at the wrong table, drank a bunch of strangers' drinks and stole my own coat.

On to the bank robbery. Two crimes happened that day. But let me tell you it was a Thursday, payday, the town was full of cash because of all the pipeliners and all the other crews that go along with them. It was also a rainy day, so the town of Kenora was right full of people. I took this time to catch up on my laundry. A few friends and I were at the Laundromat and a buddy told me that the end washing machine had the coin cover off and you didn't need to put a quarter in. So I put my clothes in but I pushed the lever too far and the machine didn't go through its cycle – it just stayed on spin dry. The owner came by and I told him his machine was broken. He looked over the situation and said, "You didn't put a quarter in, did you?" I couldn't even look him in the eye – boy I felt like a heel!

Just then, friends came in and said, "Come on with us, the bank is being robbed!" And sure enough it was! This guy put on a black mask and went in and told the bank manager that this was a robbery. He had dynamite strapped to his body and connected to a clothes pin which he held open. This is called a "dead man's switch" – if he lets go of the clothes pin it touches and sets off the dynamite. He got three hockey bags full of money and demanded someone to help carry the bags.

This was going on inside the bank. Outside the bank a crowd was growing and 40 or so police were stationed here and there on rooftops. Now WAIT!

We looked at the front of the bank for the better part of an hour and finally went in a restaurant and had pie and coffee. When we came out, they'd moved the police line back so now we were inside of it.

As we were walking out of the restaurant the robber and his helper were walking out of the bank, just three doors down. I looked at him and then KABOOM! The street filled with smoke and stank of gun powder. I didn't figure out what happened. I thought the robber blew something up for cover and was gonna come out shooting. I tried to get back in the restaurant but the owner had locked the door (looking back on it I was pushing a door that you had to pull to open – my bad).

Through all this smoke, you could see cops running and shouting *get back*. But then something else happened. Money, money of all denominations, started falling from the sky: 1's, 5's, 10's, 20's, 50's, 100's. Unbelievable! There was a whole pile of panic too! With me, it was like in the movies, everything was in slow motion and silent for a few moments. It was so surreal. I can honestly tell you what "smithereens" looks like – it was all over the stucco on the front of the bank!

A girl reached for her car door handle and there was a hunk of meat on it – looked just like pork – and she threw up and her friend was crying. My buddy was grabbing money as fast as he could when a cop came by and said, "Put it in the bag." My friend said, "Go to hell" and the cop jammed his rifle butt in my friend's stomach – he put the money in the bag. That night in the bar he pulled out a blood-stained $20 and said, "They didn't get this one. I'm keeping it forever." He got drunk and spent it that night.

What had happened was simply this – the first guy, the one that the robber needed to help carry the money, walked out of the bank, and the second guy, with the black mask and dynamite, followed behind him. They shot the second guy and he blew to bits – literally. The two bags of money were credited for saving the first guy's life. That robber mostly ended up stuck on the front wall of the Bank of Commerce. But there were parts of him everywhere. So I actually saw a man blow up 25 feet away from me – but the truth is you really don't see anything. He was there, then there was a huge explosion, then just smoke and gunpowder.

I phoned home to tell mom and dad about this extraordinary ordeal. They said they already saw it on National News. There was a helicopter there but I thought it was for his getaway. They were very relieved that I was safe – there were a few minor scrapes and bruises. They said on the news that he was a black man. I said no he wasn't – I saw his foot.

They never did find out who he was.

I really enjoyed my pipelining days. I just couldn't get over being paid that much. My first time back home in Saskatchewan I bought a brand new 1973 Dodge Duster for cash. Not a lot of kids get to do that. We had one altercation. The survey crew I was on was supposed to map out where the old and still-in-use pipeline was. We did and we did it wrong. The trouble is this: pipelines give off heat, and in the stretches where they run under ice, the ice is considerably thinner. A caterpillar went right over the existing pipeline and fell through, coming to rest on top of it! Well lotsa hollering and bellering and we all worked through most of the night but didn't get it out till the next afternoon. That puts everyone back and the big bosses came out to fire someone – that would make things right. I kid. I knew damn well they couldn't get this pipeline project done without me.

My older brother and I headed out to Ontario together. We mostly did everything together. We had the first skidoo suits – they were "one piecers" with hoods attached so the wind couldn't blow up your back. Plus they were shiny – if you fell on a mountain you would slide to the bottom.

About that time our crews got separated. I was based out of Dryden and Greg moved on to Kenora, but we would write letters to each other every five or six days – hard to believe in this day and age. One precautionary letter was funny as hell. He told me if you are relieving yourself in the woods pull the hood of your ski suit between your legs and hold it in your teeth – that way you won't shit in it!

Work on the pipeline stops for spring breakup, starting when the ground thaws out and continuing until it gets stable enough to work again. It's a good break for three or four weeks. I was looking forward to getting that big pipeline check! But Greg wasn't coming. He was going to stay behind and help Dad put the crop in. A very big, very important job.

One spring morning I saw the big boss and the second in command coming right towards me. I know trouble when I see it. They looked pretty rough and

41

sad. I can remember thinking I hope it's one of my grandparents. It wasn't. It was Greg – a single vehicle roll over. I was in shock. I went to the boarding house and packed my stuff (wasn't much) and headed back home. I didn't get too far before I picked up a hitch hiker going to Winnipeg. This guy was in his 30's and a bit down on his luck.

He figured out I was distraught. I had packed a big pipeline lunch and he ate that and did all the driving. It's a 14 hour pull from Dryden to Saskatoon. He drove me right to Saskatoon, a good 350 miles past his destination. I gave him what little money I had on me and he got out and started hitching back to Winnipeg. I don't even know his name.

It was our family's first brush with tragic death. I can only speak for my feelings on it. It was crushing. It was devastating losing a close brother, but now that I'm older I can see that it has to be 100 times worse being a parent.

I never went back east pipelining. I stayed home and helped on the farm. Little did I know my next move would be to the far north.

LEAVING

Spring of 1983

In the spring of 1983 we sold out the cattle, most of the horses and moved to the far north. My Dad said we were so far north we had to raise our own tom cats! Buffalo Narrows is primarily an Indian settlement and at first glance not very attractive. There are bars on all the windows and a lot of garbage everywhere. You get used to it. Plus, there are a lot of bugs. Big ole horse flies, the Indians call them "bulldogs," mosquitoes and, the worst of all, black flies. The first year I was waving them away the whole time and the Indians were just standing there. The next year the new white guys were waving them away and I was just standing there with the Indians. I believe that if the bugs make you nervous you give off a certain smell or pheromone. But that's just me talking. I do know this – bugs don't land on me anymore.

Right at the start I didn't even know how to spell Imperial Oil Agent and now I is one! Big learning curve coming up. I was about to get as busy as a set of jumper cables at a northern hockey tournament.

My First Fuel Haul

My father-in-law got me into this business. He was a very successful Imperial Oil fuel agent for many years. I was really looking for something. I wanted an adventure. I loved farming and livestock but I wanted to be my own boss. The agency came available way up in Northern Saskatchewan. The location and nature of the work was less than the greatest choice but the rewards were big.

My first haul was a load of gasoline to a service station on the Dillon Reserve around 50 miles away. I pumped off the load and went in the gas station. I couldn't help but notice there were eight or nine Indians in there. Then, the owner paid me in cash, right around $7000.

So here I was with two experiences that were brand new to me. First, I'd never been in a situation before where I was distinctly a member of a minority group. And second, the guy counted out the money in front of everyone and then asked if I wanted to count it myself! Hell no – I wanted to get out of Dodge with my hide! I've watched many, many Hollywood westerns and here I was wondering if I was right in the middle of one. I never saw the road going home – I was looking in the rear view mirror! I figured they'd be comin' after me over those hills – I'd seen it many times on the big screen. Looking back on it I can now see that I was worrying over nothing, but at the time I was still new to the North, and the situation definitely made me nervous.

My second haul was to Frank Bairnoff's service station in Ile à la Crosse. I loaded up my truck the night before and headed out early in the morning. I got about 10 miles out of town and ran out of gas. Now I had filled the truck's gas tank that night so what had happened was someone broke into the bulk station compound and siphoned the gas tank! Well, no problem – I got a whole load of gasoline in the big tank. I had to find a pop bottle in the ditch to pour gas in the carburetor to pump gas into the truck tank. I got that done and started the truck and it belched and smoked and sputtered. What I had failed to do was drain the hose – it was full of diesel fuel. So I had to drain the truck fuel tank and repeat the procedure. It was easier said than done and as I was wrestling with this getting the drain plug out of the tank and getting diesel fuel dripping all over me, a carload of Indians drove up to help. Well thanks, but I have it covered. An older gal said, "You blew the engine up!" No, that's not the problem. "Well then you've burned the brakes up." No, that's not it either!

Then I made another mistake – I said, "I filled it full of diesel!" She said, "Well no damn wonder it isn't working!" Grrrr.

I get the job done and head on my way. This is in the spring and when the ice breaks up off the big lakes the wind blows and pushes the ice heaves 20 to 30 feet in a pile, but I didn't know that. I reach my destination and can't find the gas station owner. Here he is at the back of his shop with a .22 rifle shooting stray dogs (a common practice in northern communities, as stray dogs are a nuisance and can be very dangerous and the odd time fatal). I get introduced, pump off the load of gasoline, get paid and then I ask, "Who's stacking up all that ice?" Well, I get the "dumbass look" and if you tell the truth most of you know that look – and no doubt have earned and received the look I'm talkin' about.

There were quite a few other hauls that were far from routine. One of 'em was to Garson Lake, a community of about 45 people on the lake near the Alberta/Saskatchewan border. You could only go in the dead of winter as there really was no road and lots of muskeg. Now we have heard or seen the show "Ice Road Truckers." Well truth is, ice is not the problem – but muskeg sure as heck is. It doesn't take freezing well and can be bottomless. That was the case with this haul. It wasn't far away but a windy, up and down hill event with the road trip being about 30 hours. So you had to bring your game face and you were on your own. We would go in in mid-February and only once was there a bit of a mishap. A front tire went down through the ice and we had to jack and pry and winch out – no big deal really.

Another haul was to Lloyd Lake Lodge, a fly-in fishing camp in the summer that needed fuel for their boats. Trouble was in the winter the place was accessible to anyone with a ski doo – which means everyone up there. So the plan was to haul the fuel in just before spring breakup and hope that the bulk of the fuel would still be there for the season. The problem was we could only go so far with the fuel truck and the balance of the way had to be ski doo'd in with 45 gallon drums. Now that's fine if it works, but the owner of the lodge always got his buddies to volunteer and there was always whiskey involved. Can you see where there might be a problem? We did manage to get that job done every year without a great deal of incident. It took a whole weekend, so you took your kit with you.

Another time a service station that also had aviation gas tanks phoned up and wanted to know if I could suck out and dispose of the aviation fuel in the tank as he believed it to be contaminated with water, and then fill the tank with new aviation fuel. We did just that but I couldn't really see anything wrong with the fuel I was to dispose of. So I disposed of it by selling it to another service station as regular gasoline. Only thing was that the owner was also a pilot and aviation gas has its own smell. Busted! So I had to come clean and we reached some sort of agreement and it all worked out in the end!

Fishing

I had never caught a fish prior to moving up north. I never went fishing. I was 30 years old when I finally hooked my first fish but turns out I was the one that got hooked! Fishing is described as a jerk on one end of the line waiting for a jerk on the other.

The fishing up north was so good you had to put your rod down to drink beer. You had to bait your hook behind a tree. An Indian up there showed me how to use a beer can, fishing line and a hook to catch fish – you tie the line to the lip of the can and use the can as the reel, wrapping the line around the can. It works – I've caught fish that way!

Here's one small story. The grocery store guy, the pharmacy guy and myself would go fishing together fairly often. We always had the same standing bet: five bucks for the first fish, five bucks for the biggest fish and five bucks for the most fish. The odd time one fish wins 'em all. This particular time there was a fish house on shore with a weigh scale. The fishing was not great and we headed to shore with one small pike each. The fish were very similar, right around four pounds each. The fish scale came in handy and those guys were tapping that scale back and forth – you would think they were weighing gold dust! While they were battling it out I looked around the shack and there were fish nets with lead weights on them. I took about four lead weights and stuffed 'em down my fish. This should solve this little conundrum. It was my turn to weigh in and I held up my fish to the scale – and it slipped out of my hand. KLUNK! My two buddies looked at each other and said, "Jackfish don't klunk!" One of the guys took his fishing knife out and opened the fish and out fell the weights. Busted!

Another time late in the fall there were four of us sitting in the boat fishing, chilly as hell and snowing. We had some whiskey with us to chase away the cold. I don't know how what happened next, happened next. The guy that worked for Sask. Power Corp. fell out of the boat. The rest of us looked at each other surprised as hell for what felt like two minutes but would actually be about three seconds. All of a sudden he came shooting out of the cold water with his arms in the air and shouted, "Don't tell my wife." That's what you were thinkin' bout down there? We got him in the boat and headed for shore, started a fire, dried him out and had lunch. I don't think his wife ever found out and probably won't unless she buys this book!

A lot of the Indians up there made their living commercial fishing using nets. That is one tough way of making a living and the guys doing it are well-suited to the job. They were tough men! I sold the fuel to these gents and it was interesting work. One of the biggest fishing outfits up there was a guy named John Hansen. John phoned me up one New Year's Eve and said come over and I'll settle up with you. I came over and John and his men were getting ready to head out across the frozen lake in the dark of night. He paid me in full, we had a shot of whiskey and I watched those men load up and head out in the dark across the lake in two sno buggies. I will never forget that sight! I watched them go across the ice until their tail lights were out of sight. Made me wonder where those tough men would find comfort out there that night!

I regret not keeping a journal on all the fishing trips we had over the years up there.

Gary Thompson

One of the guys I met up north was the helicopter pilot named Gary Thompson. He had a helicopter business and owned a Sikorsky helicopter, three Jet Ranger helicopters and a Bell 47 – the fish-bowl-looking helicopter. Gary would always say, "There's no more real characters anymore," and he was right. There are fewer and fewer every day and with every generation. In the old days every third guy was a character and that's basically what this book is about. Gary was like no one else I've ever met. This guy truly walked to the beat of his own drum. I liked him immediately.

Gary also had a V-tail Beech Bonanza. I'm not an authority on planes, I just like 'em. The V-tail was a sports car of an airplane and a little controversial as it took more flying skills than other planes. Gary took out every bump-rivet and put in flat rivets and also put in extra fuel tankage – both of these things are very illegal and dangerous but allowed you to fly faster and farther. He also put together a little "kit" plane that he would do aerobatics with. Gary would use his fleet of helicopters to fight fires in the summer and lived in St. Cloud, Florida in the winter. The reason Gary modified his airplane was so he could fly it to England, also illegal for many reasons – the single engine being one of them, along with the single pilot. He did this to purchase an airplane from the Finnish navy called a Folland Gnat. There were only 50 or so of these made, probably because they had several design flaws (although it was one of the first to experiment with an ejector seat – more on this later). Gary always wanted to outrun the F-16's at the Cold Lake airbase. Buffalo Narrows is located northeast of this vast fighter jet training facility and if you violated their air space they scramble the jets, every time. It is really something to see an F-16 on either side of your airplane – flying with its nose up and tail down to get down to your speed. If they wiggle their wings you have to follow them down to land or they have the legal right to shoot you down. Exciting, huh? I've seen them out the window twice. These air force pilots would use our vast airspace and sometimes our runway to practice "touch and goes." Every once in a while they would break the sound barrier and that is an experience that you will never get used to. Sounds like a big explosion and everything in your house or office shakes. Those boys weren't above playing the odd trick either. I was driving a fuel truck home from a delivery and an F-16 buzzed me from behind at a height of about 30 yards. I thought I was cashing in my chips! One time I saw an F-16 point straight up and keep going till he was out of sight.

Well, back to Gary. He was a true pilot. I met a lot of them and they all had one thing in common – they all absolutely loved their work. Where Gary stood alone was this: no rules applied to him. They say he looped a Norseman, supposed to not be possible but maybe Gary didn't hear that part. The Ministry of Transport was always breathing down Gary's neck for this infraction or that and so was the IRS for that matter. I lived beside Gary for seven years and he was always planning his escape. He had a bag full of Krugerrands – South African gold coins, illegal in Canada at that time because of apartheid. He had a money belt with thousands of dollars in four or five currencies and always said he was going to move to the Caymans and run a bar on the beach.

I drove Gary to the airport the day he flew himself to England. I loved the way he packed. He had a small kit bag and couldn't get his dress shoes in so he threw them over his shoulder and said, "They have shoes in England." He also had a piss jug. If it rained hard up there Gary would usually fly somewhere else – as there would not be any firefighting work. I flew out of Edmonton with him once in the middle of a storm. It was surreal to be that close to lightning and I'm OK with planes bucking up and down but sometimes we were skidding sideways – I was not fond of that. Another time my family was up and Gary was up in his Bell 47 and saw my black van driving back from the beach, so he buzzed it and then hovered in front of it on the highway – but I wasn't in it. It was my brother and mom and kids, and he scared the heck out of them.

Gary always invited me to visit him down in Florida in the winter – I never did make it but we made plans to hook up in New Orleans once and go to a Saints game. I got down there and no Gary so I phoned his wife and asked, "Where's Gary?" Her reply was, "Isn't he with you?"

Two of the bush pilots went down one winter and spent some time with him. He had a small yacht and would bump farther and farther off shore into the ocean – getting his boating skills better. They came back with a scary story. They spent the night on his boat but they were in a shipping lane and darned near got run over! I guess those ocean liners look pretty big from a small boat.

Now here is where it gets pretty interesting. Gary was flying to California to work in some movie. The Bonanza hit the ground somewhere around Shreveport, Louisiana. They had a funeral for him back in Florida but the only one not there was Gary. Now this is just me talking but I firmly believe Gary pulled a "Huck Finn." He staged his own death. He was always talking of the Caymans for years. I always said if you gave me 10 grand and two weeks I'd find him. The trail would be pretty cold now, though!

Now for a footnote. Several years later an Irish buddy and I thought we'd like to take helicopter lessons. We thought it would be cheaper if we bought a helicopter to take 'em in so my friend found a helicopter for sale online. The helicopter was at a private airport outside Denver. Off we went on a road trip. We got there and here is a Bell 47. I told the guy a friend of mine had one of these up north. We got talking and what a crazy co-incidence, here this guy had bought the Bonanza wreckage from Gary's estate (they part them out, the instruments, wiring, etc.).

Now my partner from Ireland is freaking out over this. He subscribes to the 123 official state superstitions and also the 89 unofficial superstitions. This is just too much of a coincidence for my friend to handle.

We had quite a chat and I told him my take on everything. I asked to see the wreckage. It was Gary's Bonanza alright. I asked if I could take the tin snips and cut off one of the "call letters." He said go ahead. I have it in my house. I plan on giving it back to Gary when I run into him!

We All Know This Guy

You know this fellow. Every time you have a get-together with friends and a few good stories come out this guy will top you. If you were talking how cold or how high or how big – no matter what the situation, this guy will top you.

I am going to go on a little rant now. This is why I hate BS'ers! They trivialize every story! When you are sitting around visiting and recollecting there are some people that are not in the lime light, but they have stories too and the one they just told might have meant a great deal to them to share. So when that happens and a big-mouthed BS'er tops it with his obvious BS not only is it rude and annoying it is disrespectful. Do they really think we are that dumb to believe their crap? (*Exhale*, Ernie!)

Well, I learned to get over it and myself too – so on with the story. There was a guy like that up north – we'll call him Leonard. My buddy John and I would set him up and have fun with the situation. One particular time we were going to tell him how hard we had to work and see what he had to say. I told him that I worked on a pipeline in northern Ontario and we would work 12-14 hours a day. His reply? "Oh that's nothing, I ran a caterpillar on the Alaska Highway. I got so far ahead of the crew so I just kept going. I ended up building road for 54 hours. I was so tired I got off the Cat and slept for 24 hours. When I finally woke up my tongue was like a block of wood." Well buddy, you are the king – the king of bullshit!

The trouble was every now and again he would come through on something. My friend John was a bit of a hunter so we were going to set this guy up with a big moose story. Here goes.

John: "I came upon this bull moose in the woods and his antlers were just about 60 inches wide. Supplied us with meat all winter."

Leonard: "Oh, that's nothing. I came upon two bull moose – their antlers were closer to 70 inches wide. Shot 'em both and made a chair with the antler pans."

Well, I saw the damned chair. It was beautiful. It's in his gramma's house.

Two more short stories while I'm here.

Leonard had a boy Billy, the same age as my oldest boy, about five years old. Leonard was home-schooling his kid, which was making the kid about as weird as Leonard was. One day I was looking after the kids and Leonard phoned and asked if he could drop little Billy off to play with my kids. Fine with me and he did. Well I never saw that kid again. The weird little shit hid in the house and would not come out. We had a modest two story log home; it was not very big, but I could not find that little bugger. He hid for three hours. Finally, I see his mother driving up to pick up little Billy. Put yourself in my shoes – I have no idea where he is or what I can possibly say to his mother. She knocked on the door, I opened it. Just then little Billy appeared by my side. I said nothing, but I coulda choked that little shit!

Now going back to the gramma. Her name was Julia Diagneault (a French name, pronounced Di-o – I've always maintained that if you shake a French Canadian's family tree hard enough an Indian will fall out). Anyhow, she was absolutely strikingly beautiful – five foot nothing, with beautiful long grey hair that went down to her waist. Her husband was Frank Diagneault and he was absolutely striking too, a tall handsome Cree Indian with chiselled features. They both could be movie stars! I never missed a chance to visit them. You can tell a true Indian – they point with their lips and Frank was great at it.

Now as in all small communities there are lots and lots of relatives. Diagneault was a very common name up there. There were piles of 'em and mostly just wonderful people. Hard working and handsome. Frank's grand daughter would babysit every now and again and she was delightful. I would quiz her about Frank and Julia. They had 23 children. Do I need to repeat that? Frank had about nine when his wife died and Julia had about nine when she left – on foot – with all the kids to get out of a bad situation. They hooked up and had about five kids together! I said that is simply incredible! "How long have they been married?"

She replied, "Two years."

Extraordinary people to say the very least!

So I Met Eddie Shack

I gotta say this is one of the best times I've had with my clothes on. Firstly, if you don't know who Eddie Shack is, he was a hockey star for the Toronto Maple Leafs in the 60's and 70's. Very flamboyant, he would fill the arenas with fans wanting to see his antics, a real hockey legend and hero. He even has a song written about him: "Clear the track – here comes Shack."

The Molson Old Timers came up to Buffalo Narrows to put on an exhibition game against Buffalo's finest. They were playing our Indian team and these guys are tough. Well the Molson team – 20 years their senior – made monkeys out of the local boys. At one point Normie Ullman got the puck and put on such a dipsy-doodling puck-handling display you did not notice that one by one his team mates went and sat down. There was just Normie and the rest of the other team following him like ducks. It was great.

The Old Timers got up 15 goals in no time so they said they would switch goalies, giving the home team a pro goalie. The puck was dropped at center. Eddie Shack won the draw and took the puck and sent it sailing high down to the home town's end. The goalie stopped the puck – then shot it in – now 16 to zip! They then switched the goalies back. It was tremendous entertainment.

I was with my friend Gary Thompson and said, "I know where hockey players go after a game – they go for a beer!" The only problem was the only drinking establishment in town, the "Big Buffalo," is an Indian bar and can get rough. I've been in a few very tough bars in my day and this certainly was one of them.

So away we go. Gary and I are the only white guys in the place and there are 200+ Indians. Then in walks Eddie Shack, and boy he looks like the Eddie Shack of the glory days – a big guy with a big nose, big moustache, big cowboy hat, a big sheepskin coat and smoking a big cigar. Every Indian in the place stopped what he was doing to look at him.

Eddie was at the door looking back and forth – you know this is a new one to him – and I stand up and wave him over. He looked really happy to see us. Eddie came and sat with us and pretty soon a big Indian gal came over to pick a fight with Gary – this is exactly why you don't go in that bar. She was leaning over top of Eddie Shack's head cussing Gary out. Eddie had a really funny look on his face – I wish I'd had a camera. I got up to go to the men's room – which is very dangerous – and standing next to me at the urinal is an Indian saying, "You guys are sure good hockey players," assuming I was one of them. So I say,

"Yes, we are." He says, "Which one are you?" I say, "Don't you recognize me? I'm Eddie Shack." He says, "Wow, can I have your autograph?"

Well, being the kind of guy I am of course I write out "Best wishes – Eddie Shack."

He follows me out and to my table, not wanting to let go of the moment, and I sit down next to Shack.

The Indian says, "Now wait just a minute, if you are Eddie Shack, who is this guy?"

I answer, "Don't you recognize Maurice Richard?"

So he asks Eddie for an autograph and, trooper that he is, Eddie writes out "Best wishes – Maurice Richard."

Eddie will long remember his night in Buffalo Narrows.

Wrestling

This may be the most controversial thing I say in the whole book but I gotta say it: "I strongly suspect pro wrestling to be fake." There, I said it – one less elephant in the room.

So raising four boys you end up watching – and doing – a lot of wrestling. I mean really they do put forth quite an entertainment spectacle. My friend John told me one thing you have to do is to go to a pro wrestling match live, and boy was he ever right. But somehow along the way I led my young sons to believe I could lick any or all of those wrestlers. The big day finally came. We went to the Saddledome in Calgary – a far cry from the dark little reserve of Buffalo Narrows.

Somehow my youngest boy, maybe four years old, got it in his head we were going to wrestle these guys, and he got cold feet. It took quite a lot of convincing to get him to go in. Once inside it was pandemonium. The lights, the noise, the build-up simply electrifying.

Now for the main event. The evil Yakasumo Brothers were to square off with the Gunn Brothers, Brad and "I forget." They were billed as the Smoking Gunns and wore slickers and cowboy hats. So you pretty well know who we identified with.

They start the match and our cowboys true to form are giving those evil foreigners a good thrashing. Then the referee gets in and gets one of the Gunn Brothers in the corner and is wagging his finger at him for a rules infraction. Meanwhile both the Yakasumo Brothers are in the ring beating the tar out of Brad behind the ref's back!

Well my oldest son (at that time about seven or eight) came unglued. He is on his feet hollering, "That's not fair, Ref, look behind you, look behind you!" I had never seen him react like that. But everyone raises their kids to be fair. And I will prove it – just try giving one kid a bigger ice cream cone than the other.

Anyway, I kinda escalated the situation. I stood up and was hollering too. Ref, look behind you! It's not fair it's not fair!

I said to my son Jess (five years old), "I should go down there and help those guys." And he says, "Yes, Dad, go Dad go!"

Can you imagine the headlines! The only thing I would do differently would be to spend money and get ringside seats!

57

White Water Rafting

There are two Clearwater rivers in Alberta and I've been neck deep in both of them. Two of the local bush pilots thought it would be a good idea to see if they couldn't make a side line business selling white water rafting tours. The Clearwater River starts in Saskatchewan, then flows west to the mountains (not many on this side of the Rockies head west) and hooks up with the mighty Athabasca River in Fort McMurray. Half way there are the White Mud falls.

We start this venture May long weekend. The ice is just getting off the big lakes and the water is barely above freezing. There are eight of us and two big rugged rafts. One of the pilots has a little experience at this and the rest of us not so much. Sometimes it's better this way. Ask my sons what I think of someone who introduces himself as an expert. I don't like that term – and those kinda guys remind me of that Steve Earl song about a cap and ball Colt hand gun: "They can get ya into trouble right off the get-go."

We drove up past La Loche and really got into serious trouble right off the get-go. We lowered our rafts down a cliff by a waterfall. The trouble was the waves were pushing the raft against the canyon wall and filling it with water, and it was so loud we couldn't communicate. Finally, the raft headed down the river. I jumped in, along with three other guys. But there was nothing we could do – we were adrift and at the river's mercy, sitting in ice cold water. Away we go and soon enough we hang up on a big rock. One of the guys gets out on the rock and pushes us off, but the dummy doesn't jump back in! So he's two feet away, then five, 10, then there he is standing on a big rock in the middle of the rapids. He got rescued by the second raft but to say he was not part of the solution but a big part of the problem would be very accurate.

There was not a thing we could do and down the river we go. We paddle and paddle and get to shore but in a really bad spot. The other two guys jump out but can't land the raft and down the river I go by myself! Try as I might I can't make shore. The rapids eventually play out and I'm coming up on glassy water, spray and foam and a big roar – another @x!#!? waterfall! I made the decision to abandon ship and try to swim to shore when just then a rock ledge jutted out and saved the day. I was more than a mile ahead of everyone and managed to bail the water out of the raft and get it on shore. There was a good enough little spot there for camp so I busied myself with getting wood and the tent up. Finally, everyone started showing up, half exhausted and worn out.

Now for a fish story. I said well, someone better get something for supper and I headed back to the river with my fishing rod. In two casts I landed the biggest pike I've ever caught in my life, around 20 pounds, and the second cast I caught my biggest walleye ever, around six pounds! I came walking back to camp in less than 10 minutes with my catch. Did that ever change the atmosphere – it went from being worn out to a damn stampede! They almost knocked me down getting back to the river. The funny thing was, no one else caught a fish. It was just the oddest thing. Those two fish did the job, though. That pike was the second biggest I'd ever filleted (my son caught one bigger). We were well fed that night.

The second day didn't go smooth either. We came upon a water chute that dropped eight or ten feet. Believe me, very tricky and very exciting. Our raft went first and we were heading into it sideways! That would have been disastrous. We paddled furiously and got straightened out and swoosh – we squirted through it! We were hollering and cheering and wowing! Now for the second raft. They hit the chute head on but the raft did what white water rafters call a "Colorado Sandwich" – the nose of the raft hit the bottom of the chute and then the raft folded in half! When it sprang back apart it sent the back two guys and all the gear a good 20 feet in the air! What a sight. Those guys looked like rag dolls! We spent the rest of the day gathering up the guys and the gear. Fortunately, everything was packed in river bags and we didn't lose a thing.

Those first two days put us way behind schedule for where and when we were to be picked up. The next day was cold and dreary with wet snow falling all day long. Sitting in a raft in those conditions just drains away any strength or energy you have. There was also not a single place on the river banks to dock and get a fire going and cook a lunch. We finally found a place to dock right around dark and got a fire going and made a pot of "Lipton cup-a-soup." That ranks up there with one of the best meals I've ever had – I could literally feel my strength and attitude returning.

It was a rough enough trip, lots of portaging. It was damn sure a great adventure and by the time the float plane picked us up we'd pretty well had all the fun we could stand!

Picker Truck

The Saskatchewan Power crew were up in town doing some work with a five-ton picker truck. Instead of going around on the road they decided to drive across the small bay, like everyone else. Unlike everyone else their big truck went thru the ice, with the front end poking up and just barely visible. You might say the boys screwed up a tad! The truck stayed that way for a few days while a plan was formulated (I'da liked to have been in that meeting). I told them one of my brothers was licenced to scuba dive under ice and could hook the truck up. So this is what happened: they built a big triangle frame out of timbers, positioned it over the truck and over the course of a few days hooked the truck to it.

Now this was back in the days when the standard practice of the foreman was to raise hell and holler and threaten to fire everyone. And that would make things nice and peachy. The jackass they sent up did not disappoint! Kinda reminded me of the Queen of Hearts – off with his head, off with his head. Now the SaskPower boys were on thin ice as it was (come on now – I couldn't resist!) – but I wasn't. My brother came up from the icy water and I went over to see what he wanted. The jackass is hollering at me: "What's he want?" I hollered back at him: "He needs the booster cables; we'll drive it out." Well, I got a lot of laughs from the spectators but the foreman was mad as hell!

Finally, everything was a go and they winched that truck out of the ice and it was hanging in the air from this timber frame. But it was very late now and that's where the truck spent the night. The trouble was this: as long as the truck was in the water, it was safe, but now that it was out, water had gotten into every hydraulic tank, fuel tank gas line everywhere, then froze and expanded, completely wrecking the whole truck! No one thought of that. All in all, that was a pretty entertaining few days and helped break up the winter!

John Midget and the School Marm

John Midget was a pioneer in opening up the north with airplanes. A pioneer in every sense of the word. He started C&M Airlines in La Loche, Saskatchewan. When I met him he had already made his fortune and reputation. He had sold his airline but was not content to retire.

So what he did was buy the freighting rights on Lake Athabasca and run the 80 mile ice road. He and his wife "Deductions" lived in a school bus on Lake Athabasca and maintained the ice road. His wife got her name from the bush pilots that flew for them. At the end of the season when it was time to draw up their pay she would deduct their cigarettes, booze, soup and other expenses that they had incurred over the season, always leaving them with a lot less pay than they expected.

Now there is a TV show called Ice Road Truckers. I've done all I wanted of that and never considered it glamorous. There are rules to driving a big rig on ice. Go too fast and you push a wave ahead of you and the ice breaks up on shore in front of you and you don't make it to shore. Go too slow and you cause a wave behind you and the guy behind you doesn't make it.

There are two stories that really stand out. The first one happened around the winter of 1985. Uranium City ran out of heating oil. There are three ways to get fuel in: one is shipping it by barge on the river, the second is hauling on the ice road and the third is flying it in. So it was late spring but still a full month before breakup. For you people who don't know the term, "breakup" is when the rivers literally break up – the ice goes out and the rivers flow freely.

The trouble was two-fold. Firstly, the road bans were on, which happens when the roads start thawing out – trucks can only haul at 70 percent capacity to protect the roads in that vulnerable state. Secondly, the ice road was starting to weaken and John had already pulled his tinder bridge and equipment off the ice.

Imperial Oil planned on sending seven B-train semis up there at 70 percent fuel capacity, stopping in at my bulk station and getting topped off for the rest of the journey. The execs at I.O.L got hold of John, who said he would take the caravan across the ice for $1500 per truck – triple the usual fare (boy I loved the North). The oil execs were furious – they figured they were really being taken (on the other end of it for once). They said, "Don't you have a government in northern Saskatchewan?" I told them the government on Lake Athabasca was John Midget – weigh your options.

Now on to my pay – I told them I needed $6750– about 10 times more than my standard sales commission. The Oil exec was over a barrel and finally he asked me how I arrived at that exact figure. I told him he really didn't want to know. I ran into him a couple years later at a convention and he asked me again. I told him I was holding my Visa bill at the time I was talking to him on the phone.

The second story really is pretty incredible. A fishing outfit had their sno cat buggy go through the ice. The buggy, incidentally, is a vehicle on tracks about the size of a one ton truck that can haul about four fishermen, their gear and their catch – and there it was at the bottom of Lake Athabasca in 80 feet of water. John drove up there with two Indians and a tractor and all the gear he needed and came back two days later with the sno buggy.

Now this is where it gets really interesting and shows just what can happen when determination and imagination meet. There are tall timbers on the south shore of Lake Athabasca. John cut down the exact two trees he needed. The first one was a straight tree, the second a school marm.

A school marm is a slang term for a tree split into two fairly equal trunks, like a sling shot only on a grander scale. (If you're curious about how the name came about, look up "schoolmarm tree" on Google – the story may surprise you.) Anyway, these guys fished the sno buggy with a big hook and cable and simply winched it up, anchoring the school marm in the ice and walking the other pole around and around.

Every day in the north I would witness something I'd never seen before and haven't seen since. I didn't witness this but what I did do was fuel up the guys who lost the sno buggy through the ice and fill up John's rig when they came back with the sno buggy. Amazing men!

The Snow Fort

A few years of being up north my family and I were starting to get on our feet. We lived in a little cul de sac in a double wide trailer with one neighbor named Isadore Desjarlais, plus the auto body guy, the grocery store guy, and seven members of the RCMP. They called our area the "Bay of Pigs." One day I see the grocery store guy moving furniture. I walk across the road and ask, "Gene, what are you doing?" He said he was moving to his trailer by the grocery store. Now Buffalo Narrows is built like any other northern town, all on high ground, not streets and avenues. The downtown was two miles away, and his wife wanted to be closer. Gene had the nicest house in Buffalo, a beautiful, cozy log home, whereas my trailer was where the SaskPower crew would stay, so it showed a lot of rugged wear and tear. Gene was swapping places with his butcher. I said heck, swap me places and the butcher can take my place. I said I'll write you a check and you write me a smaller one and next time we get down south we'll get a lawyer and make it legal. We shook hands and started moving stuff. He and I figured all the appliances could stay right where they were, but that didn't happen – we had to move them across the road too.

Now right at that moment in time I felt like a king. I had a happy, healthy family, a job that made a lot of money, and now a beautiful log home with a wood stove. Before, in our trailer, if the power went out (which was not unusual) we would have to drain the hot water tank and bundle the little kids up and head to a neighbor who had a wood stove. Not no more! I would burn pine in the day time, the wood would snap, crackle, and pop, and an armload of birch would keep the chill off for the whole night. I'd get up a little earlier than the kids and get the fire going well so it would be toasty warm when the kids woke up.

Now getting back to that check I wrote. It was more than double the check I received. I was with the same bank but there was a new bank manager. He said that was not the proper way to conduct business and wouldn't honor my check! Well thank goodness Vern the banker came to my rescue and smoothed 'er all over. I so have to mention that stove one more time. It was a great fixture with a glass door with wolf pictures etched into the glass. But I was not raised with wood heat and it took a while before I was comfortable with a roaring fire in the middle of our home.

We had our first Christmas in that little log home and the old in-laws came up. I don't know how to word this but our situation was not what they were used to down south. We had to work all Christmas day and three of the fuel hauls were to service stations – all cash. Between my one driver, Napeau and me, I ended up taking roughly $30,000 cash home! I set the money down on top of the television as if it wasn't unusual (it was) just to get a reaction. They were worried if we would be safe with that in the house. The routine way to handle that was every night I would go to Hudson's Bay Company, give them the cash, they wrote me out a bank draft and I mailed it to my bank in Saskatoon. I didn't want anyone to know that I had any cash at all.

Now about that snow fort. I started building the fort in the yard for the kids, and the project got away on me. I was taking time off work to build this thing, it even had an upstairs floor and a long tunnel. The kids and I had a lot of fun with it. I even told the kids it had a secret room. There really wasn't a secret room – what I would do was tell them to go around the house and I would hide in it and when they came to look for me I would go around the other side of the house and watch them trying to find me!

Now I want to say a little about my fuel hauler, Napeau. He was as steady a man as you could ask for. There was just one problem – there was one house he couldn't deliver fuel to: his girlfriend's. Turns out his wife and his girlfriend didn't get along. Napeau turned up at the office before Christmas with a beautiful pair of handmade moosehide and wolf-fur beaded mitts – a work of art. The mitts stayed in the office for weeks. I finally asked him about it. He told me his girlfriend had made them for him and that his wife would recognize her work so he couldn't take them home. You see, all the native girls had their own patterns they used and also their choice of colored beads, as unique to them as your name is to you. I said, "Give them to me, my bride can't read beads!"

I guess I spilled the beans on old Napeau. I can only hope that neither of those gals buys this book!

The $5000 Game of Cribbage

So I played a $5000 game of crib (this little chapter could be named a few things).

My friend John and I would get together and play cards, usually crib. We would play for money and over the course of eight years neither of us really hurt each other. Meaning almost never would the debt be over 100 bucks. We would side bet and tease each other.

Now we also both talked a great game of golf and planned on actually golfing with each other one day. I always said I was going to see what he was made of on the golf course. I do maintain this – before hiring someone or working for someone you should golf 18 holes with him. Believe me, it will reveal a lot about a person's character.

My plan was simple. I was going to wait until John had about a 10-15 foot putt, then stick a $100 bill near the hole and let him try to make the putt. My plan worked perfectly! No one could have tried harder than John but alas he missed the putt.

The fact is I wasn't really putting up much. If he had made the putt – he was buying! And if experience has taught me anything – I know I can eat enough steak and lobster and drink enough wine to cover 100 bucks.

The real reason we went out to North Battleford was not for the golf game. My dad would take cattle to butcher and sell 30 or so heifers every year. Most people would buy half a side of beef and tell the butcher how to cut it up. You know – how big for the roasts, how many pounds of hamburger in a pack, etc. So John and I each bought a half side of beef and drove out to North Battleford to pick it up. We just threw the golf game in the trip.

Seldom did we get to go out together so when these occasions arose – you really made 'em count. Hence the golf game and the restaurant meal and the imbibing after.

We got out of the restaurant pretty late and started heading back to Buffalo when it dawned on us we hadn't picked up the meat – the whole damn reason for the trip.

We phoned the butcher – woke him up – explained our situation – we were drunk and a little dim-witted – and he agreed to meet us and get us our meat.

This time on our way out of town we got in the wrong lane – instead of heading straight out on the highway we got siphoned off on the clover leaf, going way too fast. We hit the guard rail with John's old Chevy half-ton – hard! But miraculously we hit it with the front and back bumper only. No damage to the truck. We bounced back and came to rest. The only harm was some of the meat flew out in the ditch. It took a bit but we got it all and continued on our journey.

That night we stayed at John's parents, about half way home. Now John's dad was a wine collector – and, coincidentally enough, we were wine drinkers. We drank a lot of wine that night and played a lot of cards.

Well I got on a winning streak and couldn't lose. We started doubling and doubling the stakes. We couldn't go to bed with him owing me thousands of dollars. We finally had to play a game for $5000 and he finally won, thank god – it was about 3 in the morning. After all that it was $5017 – something like that – so in the end I owed him 17 bucks. That peeved me off!

The next day we set off – not a far drive, about four hours or so north – with the worst hangover ever.

We stopped in Meadow Lake for a drink. This was the first time I'd ever seen a Slurpee and gulped a bunch down. That may have been the single worst experience in pain I have ever had! I thought my head would explode. That I guarantee you is something you only do once.

Pine Channel Gold Corp

In my seven-plus years in the North not a lot changed work-wise. You hauled heating oil in the winter and aviation fuel in the summer to fight forest fires. There was one exception. An outfit from Vancouver bought 100 drums of helicopter fuel one year and started marking out a grid 100 miles north of us. The next year they did the same but also put in a small camp and had a small caterpillar up there pushing a little dirt around. The third year they did the same but started up a drilling rig too. Now when you hear drilling, you immediately think oil but these guys were taking core samples for precious minerals – gold.

Buffalo Narrows lies smack dab between Big Peter Pond and Churchill Lake but also right between the legendary tar sands and the great Canadian Shield. But to my knowledge it is also where the oil reserves have run out and the gold deposits haven't begun.

So finally after three years the guy who has been writing checks for fuel is standing in my office. I'm very interested in his business and futures and ask, "Are you guys on the stock market?"

"Yes, we're on the British Columbian Exchange"

"Well, should I be buying stock?"

"Absolutely, but buy this week as we are planning a press release and the stock should rise quite significantly."

I did what I'm fairly good at, I procrastinated. Firstly, I was pretty darn busy at work and now I also had four little boys all under five years old at home.

Secondly, till now I never had any money to even think about the stock market, plus I really didn't even know the first thing about buying them. My accountant sorted me out and I got hold of a stockbroker the next week. I asked what are Pine Channel Gold stocks at? I figured I could gamble with 10,000 bucks! He said they were at 40 cents. What were they last week? Eighteen cents – so I kinda missed the boat a bit! I was still hauling fuel to this guy, little top-ups here and there, and the shares went up to $1.40 over the course of the winter. Then they fell back down to 40 cents. What the heck, I threw my hat in the ring.

Then things started going sideways. Spring had arrived, but as always in the North it came late and stayed on. There are different grades of diesel fuel for different weather conditions: really thin diesel for burning in the sub-arctic temperatures, and then, for summer conditions, mid-grade and thicker diesel with higher octane, which gave better mileage.

I was already stocking and using mid-grade diesel, and I sent 100 drums of it up to the camp. The Vancouver guy said it gummed up his drilling rig and cost him a lot of down time. He also said he was not going to pay for that fuel (and of course the freight) as it was a minimum delivery.

As quick as humanly possible I got 50 drums of light winter grade fuel up there. I was figuring this is the only new business happening up here in years and I don't want to screw this one up! Then he phones up and says his men mixed the drums up and he's still in a fix. Now I can't help that and I'm starting to smell a big rat! I told him get your guys to pour it in a pail first, if it pours freely it's winter grade, use it at night; then burn the heavier fuel in the day time when it's several degrees warmer. Then his camp burns down, he gets paid insurance plus he gets another benefit – he has no expense of hauling the camp out. The guy is a shyster and there never was any gold. I was selling my shares but now no one is buying. I get out of that part not too scratched up but he's not going to pay me for the fuel. I still have an ace in the hole, though – all those empty fuel drums have a $30 deposit paid on 'em and they are no value to him – just me. Wouldn't you know, though, that rascal was ahead of me there too. He hired the Indians to tidy up the mess, but instead of paying them he gave them the drums – which meant that I had to fork out my own cash to get them back. Pine Channel Gold Corp slipped right off the board. Can't win 'em all!

Cowboy Picture.

My brother Robert on the bank of the Nile river.

Me and my four young sons skiing.

My son and my dad with a big pike.

The Century Family Farm Award.

Fly-in fishing at Buffalo Narrows.

My son skiing.

Me and my brothers at the Radisson fair.

My prize saddle – a Mawson Brothers original.

National Champion quarter horse stallion.

My AQHA Champion Stallion.

Setting up camp.

Shed hunting.

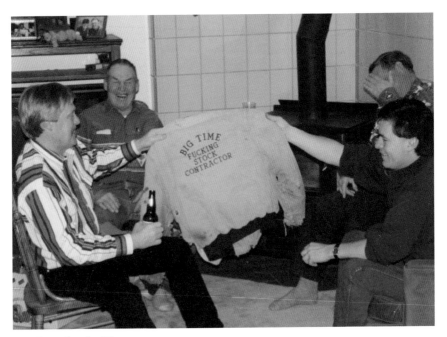

Trophy jacket for Harv.

Selling the Rocky Mountain House Auction Mart.

Branding at Rex's.

Me and the boys.

Home sweet home.

Everet, Charlie and Albert. Three "Amigos" in camp.

"Hard Water".

Elk hunt.

Trophy cabinet.

Back in camp.

Five years of sheds from the same two deer.

Saskatchewan Monarch.

The author.

In Loving Memory Of

Braden Scott Lamar Nutting
1996 - 2010

In Loving Memory.

The author.

LIVING THE
DREAM

Moving

Moving is an unsettling time, especially big moves. There are many folks who won't relate to this but there are a lot of you out there who will. To make a big move – changing jobs, continents, situations – takes courage and an adventurous spirit. It's especially unsettling on little kids. When we moved out of the North to cowboy country in western Alberta my four little boys did not quite understand why that had to happen. I'd purchased a pretty darn nice little ranch and start setting up the place. It started to feel like home a bit when we unpacked the fridge magnets and put the pictures up. My one son said, "Dad, who moved our kitchen here?" My brother Mitch helped out driving the moving truck and I had two-way radios hooked up so our caravan could keep in touch. The boys and Mitch kept up the banter pretty near non-stop with the boys asking questions like, "Who would win a fight between an eagle and a badger?"

Now here's a story within a story. This one is called "Be careful what you say around a six-year-old." As I said, the boys were pretty apprehensive about the move and to quell their fears I told them we were moving west to be cowboys with horses and cows – the works – which we did. The eldest son (Carson, age six) said, "Dad, what do you know about being a cowboy?"

My reply was, "Well, pretty well near everything you need to know!"

"Well, *are* you a cowboy?"

And so it went.

Time went on and we got settled in and my oldest boy went to grade one. The grade one teacher – and by the way, it should be mandatory that every grade one teacher should write a book – they would all be best sellers, every one of 'em. Her name was Mrs. Shippelt, what a gal, the right person for the right job. Her family was long connected with pony chuck wagon racing, one of the most thrilling, hair-raising sports in the world. The name "pony" is kind of a misnomer, as the horses are smaller thoroughbreds that can split the wind. I love this sport as much as I love rodeo – and I love rodeo! I got to help out, first as a barrel judge, then as a mounted track judge (and let me tell you, if you're not on a fast horse you're literally left in the dust) and finally I got to help with the announcing duties. These crazy wagon drivers go from town to town racing their horse teams at full throttle, thrilling racing fans all across the country. The fun turns up when the wagon drivers come to town.

Whoa – back to my story! So I'm at my fuel business in the office and there happened to be a few local boys – one is my neighbor Harv, who you will hear about later, having coffee. In walks Mrs. Shippelt and she asks, "Are you Ernie Nutting?"

"Yes I am."

"So you're Carson's dad?"

"Yes I am."

"Then you must be the king of the cowboys!" And she left, laughing her head off. And so did everyone else in my office. I never really did live that one down! And every time I think of it I laugh myself. And by the way – that was my second choice for the title of this book: "The King of the Cowboys."

The joke of it is this: there is not an ounce of brag in a real cowboy. And I've heard this said a time or two also: it's hard to spot real cowboys from the road. True cowboys let their actions speak for them, not their words.

See Dad, We're Eating for Nothing

This story is for all you Dads out there who know the real meaning of spending all those early mornings (almost always in the cold) with your sons and daughters hunting and fishing. There is no more noble activity.

When we started fishing up north I had to tie my youngest kid in the boat. He was so little and like all kids that age – top heavy.

Firstly, let's go on a little rant, shall we:
- If you don't like guns, don't buy one.
- If you don't like hunting, don't go hunting.
- If you don't like tattoos, don't get one.
- If you don't like gay marriage, don't marry a gay.
- If you don't like your rights being stripped away from you, don't take away other people's rights.
- And so on!

There are many, many horrendous shootings but show me one, just one, that would have been prevented by gun control – I dare ya. It doesn't work, never will. My 30/30 is in my closet and my shells are near and that gun hasn't killed anyone. The only people that put anything in the hunting game are the hunters. All the anti-hunting lobbyists do is complain. It made me physically sick when Cecil the lion got shot and the anti-hunters went nuts. This was a greater outcry than when the terrorist group Boko Haram stole 300 school girls and sold them into sex slavery! What a bunch of I don't know whats! Just shut up and stay out of it!

Do you want to know how to save the "White Rhinoceros?" Charge $90K to hunt 'em – in five years you will have to spray for them! Right now if they stomp a farmer's turnip patch he'll get rid of him. So get over yourselves.

All our good friends at the Fish and Wildlife, I just don't get it. The hunters are the last people on earth who would like to see the end of the bears, elk, cougars, moose, whatever.

A few years ago my good friend Joe and my son Joe's 13 year-old-boy and another friend were up in the Kananaskis Park legally hunting big horn sheep when a grizzly bear started stalking their horses. This bear had been caught and collared years earlier and the collar was digging into his neck. This in all likelihood was the cause of the bear's aggressive behaviour, but whatever the cause it was the bear's death warrant – Joe ended up having to shoot him at close range. He and my son made the five hour trip down the mountain to report this to the park rangers. The next day they arrived and, at the instigation of their leader, David Hanna, laid out a forensic crime scene and charged Joe with five counts of shooting the bear with a $100,000 fine for each count. Can you say, "Overkill, dunce, moron!" This fine hung over our heads (Joe's, really) till the court date. I was in Texas at the time when I got the call, "Dad we're in real trouble this time," which is really how almost every call between me and my sons begins!

He told me what had happened and I remember saying, "You boys better get your stories straight," and Carson replying, "We don't need a story; we didn't do anything wrong!" In the end that's what saved 'em.

The court session finally began, at the little town of Canmore just outside Banff National Park. Everyone was there, even this old geek named Jim Passot, who wears jackets with elbow patches and a beard and tries to pass himself off as a defender of the bears – we were in the belly of the Greenpeacers, and *they* were hunting *us*.

It was like a wedding, all the Parks people on one side and about eight of us on Joe's side. As the news cameras were there they made our side walk through a metal detector. It was just one monkey short of a circus.

It started with a young parks warden who officially laid the charges – Dave Hanna did not have enough courage to go in case things went sideways! And they went sideways pretty quickly as the young warden had zero experience with grizzly bears and started stuttering and stammering. He was in over his head, so big ole Dave Hanna took the reins – and he was like Moses to his disciples. Now this part is rich – and you can download the transcripts Hanna said to the judge: Three things you have to realize about grizzly bears:

They aren't dangerous.

They are completely predictable.

They don't even eat meat.

Read that again!

The judge, the Honorable John Reilly, said, "Now wait a moment, they did an autopsy on that bear and there was bone and sinew in his stomach; does that not indicate that he eats meat?"

Hanna: "No – it indicates that he eats bone and sinew."

It went on like that for quite a while with that pompous ass Hanna not answering any direct question and expounding the benefits of his personal grizzly bear training program. Just simply asinine. Then he left. The second in

73

command took up the fight and court went on all day. You could tell the tide was changing after Joe and my son got on the stand.

Before the judge gave his decision he said Hanna was the worst witness he ever had on his docket, and the second in command was the second worst witness he'd ever had on his docket and he pointed to my son and said, "And you, young man, are the best witness I've ever had on my docket!"

Finally, the judge had had enough. He banged his gavel. Count 1 – dismissed. Count 2 – dismissed. Count 3 – dismissed. Counts 4&5 – dismissed.

Of course there was relief but no real closure. The wardens didn't learn a damn thing and the hunters learned not to report anything ever. Shortly after that my 88-year-old friend and his 91-year-old-partner were hunting bush partridges (legally) and were stopped parked in their truck having lunch and a beer each. A sharp-eyed resource officer saw this and gave them a $200 ticket for open liquor. I feel safer already knowing the common sense and vigilance of these brave public servants.

Now back to fishing and hunting. I have without a doubt spent 300 nights in a canvas tent with my sons – some of the best times of my life. We started out on the thin side with gear but as we went along got better sleeping bags, fishing rods, camping gear, rifles, hunting bows and on and on. My son Ben finally shot his first deer. We field dressed it, took the meat to the butcher shop, bought some pork and got jerky, pepperoni and sausage made – cost a fortune.

Now the big moment came. We are having Ben's deer meat for supper. Ben is beaming in the knowledge he is supplying the family meal. He looks at me and proudly announces, "See Dad, we're eating for nothing!"

Uncle Brosi

I really don't know where to begin with this. Brosi is not my uncle – his dad and my granddad were brothers – but somehow he and I formed a special connection and I don't know how to explain that further. We just always enjoyed each other's company. I believe he admired my cowboy ways and I always admired his character, humor and insight through life's many challenges.

Brosi went through college, got a law degree and went on to be Chief Justice of the province of Saskatchewan and in between was the lawyer for the city of Saskatoon. For you people from the south who are reading this, I'm still writing in English – Saskatoon is a city in a province in the middle of Canada.

Brosi and I always had a mutual admiration. Through all his life experiences and mine we have kept that, even though we don't always stay in touch. It's one of those deals that no matter how long the stretch we pick up where we left off.

Brosi got married three times – I guess he just liked that "new wife" smell. He had four beautiful daughters from his first bride, another beautiful daughter and a Down syndrome boy, who didn't get to stay with us all that long – a shooting star – brightened everyone's life for the short time he spent with them. And finally his third and current wife with whom he shares another beautiful daughter. His last wife is French Canadian, although you would never know it – she still has all her fingers! (You know – the French Canadians lose one or two due to logging and wood cutting incidents.) I've enjoyed their company more and more through the years.

One particular time in the 90s I came out from Alberta to haul cattle to market in Saskatoon. I had made arrangements to stay with Brosi and Noella that evening. Now between our farm and Saskatoon flows the mighty North Saskatchewan River, and across it was the dreaded Borden Bridge, lodged at the bottom of two high river banks and about 20 feet too narrow. Whenever I got to the top of the bank I would look to see if any semis were coming from the other side and try to time it so I wouldn't meet 'em on the bridge.

On this particular frosty November morning I was driving a one ton dual axle truck towing a 24 foot cattle trailer packed tight with yearling steers. The road was a little slick with frost and I was going way too fast – the trouble with one ton trucks is they have all the power to pull a load but not enough brakes to stop the load. I crested the hill and the new bridge is in sight. Now comes the second worst co-incidence in the world. I had managed to time my cattle haul at the exact same time they were officially opening a brand new Borden Bridge to replace the old one. There were a dozen vintage cars, three camera crews, four or five police cruisers and of course various political dignitaries. I came barreling over that and just when you think it couldn't get any more complicated or worse – it did.

My trailer brakes quit working. They were fine the day before – honest! Every time I touched the brakes the truck and trailer would jack knife – just a bit! This was a disaster looking to happen. I kept feathering the rig slower but went by this whole crowd way, way too fast with people waving and shouting – I expected a cop to stand out in front and put his hand up for me to stop. Then I'd have a decision to make. I made it past them all, just doing what needed done and when the panic mode stopped and I was heading up the slope past the bridge my leg was shaking like a dog's. Nobody died that day! Believe me, the situation was that tight!

One year I talked Brosi into leading the Radisson Parade with me, on horseback. That was a privilege I had for many, many years and I loved doing it. After Brosi assisted me that year I tried to stick him with the moniker "the hangin' judge." Couldn't get it to stick (I secretly think he just didn't hold up his end).

Now I don't want the next part to sound too much like the "Dukes of Hazzard" but with this many boys and a circuit judge, well, it's just a matter of time before they have to meet "professionally."

My brother Tony got tight and parked Dad's half ton truck so deep in Jack Murphy's bush we had to borrow chains to pull it out. Tony got home somehow that night and the next day Dad and I went and got the truck. Tony was charged with leaving the scene of an accident and had to go to court. Brosi's buddy and fellow judge Dick Kusi was presiding and found Tony guilty and charged him 57 bucks.

When court was said and done, Brosi brought Dick out to the farm for lunch and coffee. Just as they were about to leave Mom presented Dick with a bill for 57 bucks for lunch!

Our meetings invariably took place at the Radisson Fair – over the years that's been the gathering place for family and friends. Over the years I've had several jokes with Brosi being on the "joke" end. He solved all that at the fair one year. This lady was selling baby rabbits, and Brosi asked my young son if he would like one, just like that sign I have always gotten a kick out of: "Any unattended children will be given a free kitten." Well thanks a bunch, "Bros." We got back to my ranch in Alberta and there was a bunny cage of sorts. The first night the bunny got out or something got in – anyway, no baby bunny in the morning. The search was on, with all four little boys and me out there looking. Finally, one of my sons hollers, "I found him, I found him." Oh good, trouble over. "But him's doesn't have a head."

That didn't get me off the hook, though. Our very thoughtful neighbor brought over another *@#! rabbit, and I had to up my game. I took two days off work and welded up the best little rabbit cage you've ever seen. Around the same time someone dropped off a tame rabbit at work. I tried to get the truckers to catch him and take him home before my little boys saw him. Didn't happen. The boys showed up and had that rabbit caught in moments. Now the funny thing about rabbits is this. A boy rabbit and a girl rabbit will get along, a girl rabbit and another girl rabbit will get along. Two boy rabbits, they call 'em bucks, not so much. You know how they fight? I'll tell ya. They jump up as high as they can, bite on to each other and kick each other with their hind feet on the way down – while they both make a high pitched squeal. Scary as hell! So who the heck knows how you "sex" rabbits? We just threw them together and this crazy scary fight broke out and I headed for the hills! My eight-year-old son waited till they jumped up again, grabbed 'em both, pulled 'em apart, and took the little one out of the cage – I was gonna do that!

Through all the trials and tribulations Brosi still has the love and admiration of his big family: wife, daughters, sons in law and grand children. That is not that common, and it's wonderful to see!

So I Had Horses in the Movies

They shot the movie "Texas Rangers" near Indus, Alberta, which is just south of Calgary and very near to where the Bow River joins the Highwood. A beautiful location with high rolling hills. The movie was shot in June, and June weather in the foothills can bring anything, snow, rain, hail, sleet, and the weather did not let us down.

They needed a lot of horses, and in fact there were around 300 on the set. But they also needed horses that were broke enough to handle gun shots and all kinds of scary and spooky activities. I think I mentioned that horses have a lot of the same traits humans do. There are horses that make a big deal of every little thing and horses that shut out the trivial distractions and pay attention only to the important stuff. Nervous trainers produce nervous horses, impatient trainers produce impatient horses, etc.

The horses I brought could handle most or all of the goings' on. I auditioned them and some of my horses were put on the pay roll. They mainly used my horses for close ups of shootings and things of that nature. A movie consultant, an actual Texas Ranger named Juaquin Jackson, a six-foot-six Texan, liked riding my big red horse Bud cause the horse fit him better than most. My ole kids' horse Jake was used mostly for close ups of bad guys getting shot off their horse. It was certainly different, although a big part of it was "hurry up and wait." Oh, I better mention the first day driving to the set. I was hauling six head of horses from my ranch to the movie set but had to stop in the middle of the town of Sundre and witness the old movie theatre burn to the ground. The fire fighters were there and really quite a commotion, considering it was 4:00 am in the morning. Isn't it funny that antiquated outdated buildings that occupy prime real estate always seem to catch fire in the middle of the night? Just saying!

Now there is a lot of bullshit that goes on with making a movie, but for the first while I didn't mind because it was new and interesting. Randy Travis was in it and I was his wrangler for a few days. My job was to make sure harm didn't come his way when he was on a horse. Most movie guys need this service, although Randy not so much as he was an accomplished horseman. He was also a decent fellow. One night they worked a little late and Randy missed his first ride so he was visiting with the coffee girl. Randy is charming and gentlemanly and the coffee girl was thrilled with this. I was just sitting on my horse; my day was through when Randy got his ride home. A new kid came riding up and hadn't seen Randy before and was excited about this too. He said to me, "Why that's … that's …" I said, "Yes it is, that's Clint Eastwood." Randy laughed and said, "I'm going to get you for that, Ernie!"

The next day when they broke for lunch Randy kicked his horse into high gear and raced up the hill to the lunch tent. I had to keep up! The boss of the outfit caught up with me and said, "If I catch you pulling that sh*t again I'll fire you!" Randy was grinning – we were back to even!

Another thing I remember was that part of the movie was shot on pasture land that hadn't been used in years, and there was plenty of old dry grass – a real fire hazard. Up till that time I could count on one hand the number of new baby deer I'd seen, but in the short time there I saw over 20. There were deer and their fawns everywhere. But you had to know where to look. One day they set the camera up not 20 feet from a new baby fawn with the mother not 20 yards away in a little thicket fretting away – and not a soul noticed!

They had around 100 longhorn cows on the set and it was our job to look after 'em and every once in a while try and keep them held as a back drop for a scene and sometimes string 'em out single file to make it look like 1000 and then fall back and let the actors take over. A friend and I were in charge of looking after the cow herd for a few days and most of the time it was uneventful. But one day a helicopter landed with the brass from Universal Studios. Apparently there were some glitches – they spent roughly $40 million making this "epic" and grossed under one million. Anyway, I was on one side of the herd and my partner was on the other side having himself a nap. One of the head honchos saw him sleeping and said, "As long as that guy is sleeping he has a job, but as soon as he wakes up, fire him!"

Another time they spent all day long shooting a guy out of a tree. They dug a big four-foot-deep hole and put cardboard boxes and quilts in it for him to fall in. The next day they turned the camera around and shot some different scene. But the big hole was still there. There were about eight of us hanging around sitting on our horses and one guy said, "Can you get your horse to jump in that hole?" No one could. The hole was fairly deep but I kicked ole Bud and in he jumped. I figured I'd get out somehow, so I wouldn't be there this time next year. It was quite a struggle but we managed to scramble outta there.

I was on that movie set for 30 days. Sometime later I even saw the movie. I hardly recognized a single thing. Apparently they went back to Hollywood and re-shot pretty well the entire movie!

Caroline

One of many real characters I've met along the trail was an Irish immigrant named Roy. We got along right off the bat. I really enjoyed hearing his stories and perspectives. I mean really, I've moved around a bit and had my share of adventures but I did not cross an ocean to begin a new life. But at least he could speak the language – kinda.

We both enjoyed the same things and had several road trips together. His oldest boy and my oldest boy were the same age and we spent many long hours with hockey, 4-H, hunting and all that it takes to raise kids in general.

I could fill a book with our adventures but I'm just going to tell this one. Our sons grew up with a love of camping and the outdoors and they have become fine young men because of it.

Every May long weekend the boys would head out to the mountains and camp and party. This can be a particular volatile time in the Rockies, weather-wise. The boys and all their friends headed out west to camp and Saturday afternoon Roy and I hooked up and were going to track 'em down and see how they were making out. Now the West out there is full of oil lease roads and literally dozens of places they could be camping, so we prepared for anything – we bought 12 beers! We drove here and we drove there and didn't run into their camp. We'd each drunk three beers and stopped on an oil lease to relieve ourselves. We were standing in front of the truck peeing and wouldn't you know it – a member of the RCMP showed up out of nowhere and let the lights flash. Well, busted!

He said our two options were this: 1) we could blow in the breathalyser and be free to go or suffer the consequences; or 2) take a 24 hour drivers licence suspension and be done with it.

Well, Roy, was the driver and the penalty for being over the limit is steep. We decided to phone Roy's daughter and her and her friend picked us up and drove us and our truck back to town. The officer waited till they came and found us and we had a good visit.

The officer explained to us – I'm gonna write you out a ticket and you are going to give me your license and tomorrow you come to our office in Rocky Mountain House and you give me the ticket and I give you the license. Fair enough?

We get a ride back to town and go to the saloon for supper. On the way I look at the ticket the officer gave Roy. In the observation column he wrote "Stopped when parked with open liquor while urinating."

When we get in the saloon I whisper to Roy's daughter, "Give me the keys." She replies, "No, you've had as much to drink as Roy." I said, "Just give me the damn keys."

I sneak out to the truck and take the ticket and I can almost not write what I wrote from shaking with laughter. Under where it said "Stopped while urinating" I wrote "Plus driver has unusually short pecker" and put it back in the glove compartment.

Well, Roy's wife and another couple come into town and they go their way and I head for home. Roy's wife said, "So you and Ernie got into a little fix with the law today?" Roy said, "Not really" and explained the situation. She said what does the ticket say and Roy replied, "I don't know, never read it." Roy's wife finds the ticket and reads it aloud. Three of them in that truck cannot believe what they are hearing, but Roy can – he knows exactly what happened and is roaring with laughter!

The next day Roy is up in the police station in Rocky Mountain House. He presents the 24 hour suspension ticket to the gal working reception. She routinely takes it, puts it on a pile and hands Roy his license.

Roy says, "Wait one minute, I take big offence to what that officer wrote about me." At the time there were three officers standing in the office. The gal said what was it you found so offensive? Roy said, "Well read it – aloud!"

The gal read, "Stopped while urinating – plus driver has unusually short pecker." The officers doubled over laughing – they knew damned well that that was not written by one of their members. One of the guys grabbed the ticket and said to Roy, "Here – you better take this home and frame it!"

The $50,000 Dog

Several volumes can be written on this subject alone. You can get along with everyone but the neighbor beside you. Actually I've been very lucky in this regard but there is one little instance that deserves to be put in print.

My one neighbor was more or less an expert on horses and dogs, kids and life in general, and more for that matter and took it upon herself to look after a dog for the RCMP. Not living raised in the country she did not follow the rules of keeping your dogs at home – not letting them roam the country getting into mischief. Needless to say her dogs roamed.

The police dog got over to my other neighbor's place and when he opened his door there was the dog, a German shepherd, aggressively growling at him, not letting him out. Remember now we are not only in the country but the back woods country. The next time he opened his door the dog is still there snarling away – the only difference is this time my neighbor had his shot gun. I don't have to tell you what happened next.

Well the you-know-what hit the fan. There is a saying in the country about dogs that don't stay home and roam the country raising hell – shoot, shovel and shut up! The first neighbor reported the incident as a malicious act to the police. The police treated the matter as if the dog had been a member of the force and made life proper hell for my poor neighbor.

Of course this caused hard feelings and strained relationships in the neighborhood – a completely normal and natural occurrence – every now and then you need something like this to clear the air a little.

A while later, in the coffee shop, you-know-who was saying how terrible a crime it was to shoot the dog and that the dog would have been worth $50,000 if allowed to carry out its life raising pure bred German Shepherd pups for the police force.

Well, I could not keep my lip buttoned. I piped up and said, "You know, I'm the only guy alive that knows how to get $50,000 for a dog." (WAIT FOR IT – the restaurant fell silent.)

You gotta trade him for two $25,000 cats!

Rocky Mountain House Auction Mart

I met Clayton Cole and his dad R.C. at the James River Horse Palace sale. We became good friends and my dad and Clayton's dad became good friends also. They had a mutual interest in the cattle business and 4-H. All of my boys were in the 4-H beef club and my dad would come up every year to watch. The Coles would donate their time, energy and expertise every year – real community men.

I remember exactly when we met at the sale – Clayton was selling horse feeders. Now an auctioneer starts high and then drops till he gets a bidder. He started the feeders off at 300 bucks and got no takers, dropped 'er to 50 bucks and I started the bidding. Eventually, after lots of bidding, everyone dropped out and I got the feeders for the original ask of $300. Clayton turned to me and pointed, "Sold – and thanks for the practice."

The Rocky Auction Mart was an institution and a gathering spot for the whole community. Every Saturday morning that was the place to be. They ran a fair and square place for many years. R.C. would start off every sale by selling a pitch fork – that was his signature. All the folks would come out of the hills and consign their junk and so would their neighbors – each going home with treasures. There were lots of sights and sounds and lots of laughs – Clayton, you should put a book together!

Once a month was the horse sale. Now that was well worth going to! I've always felt if you can't sell a horse out of your yard the auction was a good place for 'em – you weren't guaranteed a price but you were guaranteed 'em gone!

Time caught up with that institution and the land got to be worth more than the business. It was pretty clear that it was time to sell it. At that time, I'd taken my real estate license and R.C. said to Clayton, "Well if we have to sell it, we may as well get that young Ernie Nutting to do it!" I was about 45 at the time.

I listed the place for sale. The auction mart had the three most important things in real estate going for it: Location! Location! Location! There were real mixed emotions about this as a lot of memories were made in that place. A few jugs of whiskey got drunk after every horse sale and great stories swapped. Rex was mad at me: "You're selling my favorite saloon!"

Shortly after I went to a small city for a wedding. I wrote down about 25 businesses on the main drag and contacted them all. Got no bites. I was walking out of a restaurant later and a grocery super store was there. I walked in, introduced myself to the manager, found out who was their property manager, and that person eventually turned out to be the buyer. But it was a long road. The auction mart pavilion really had no value, a fact I had to keep to myself as the seller would disagree strongly! It sat on 17 acres, most of which was peat moss and bog. The deal took eight months, but just because it took that long to complete the due diligence to see if the buyer could make it fit his purposes. We eventually got the deal done, with both parties satisfied.

The last horse sale was bittersweet. It was the only time I've ever bought a case of whiskey. Gonna party after. I headed over to Rex's and we loaded five head of horses and headed out. The sale came and went and we headed upstairs, along with a pretty big crew to get that whiskey drunk. It was a big job but we got 'er done! I said to Rex, "You're gonna have to drive home as I'm pretty drunk." Rex replied, "Well I'm drunk too – but I'd rather ride with a drunk man than a tired man." "Well Rex I'm drunk *and* tired!" Common sense prevailed and we started the truck, cranked up the heat and had a good sleep.

Soon afterwards they demolished the place, nothing but memories left. There's a shopping mall there now.

2:30 pm, Saturday, August 24, 1990

For a guy who really doesn't remember dates very well, I've really got this one pretty well nailed. This was the exact time that I met an older gent who likely had the biggest impact on me and my four sons.

I had just moved out of the North and bought a beautiful little ranch in the foothills of Alberta. There was a horse sale at the James River Horse Palace – sounds pretty fancy but it was just a pretty nice riding arena. I took my oldest boy with me, he was six years old – and headed to the sale. These auction sales start with the junk and small stuff, with the main event being the horses. So we watched and watched (and, oh by the way, this was also when I met another good friend and his dad, Clayton and R.J. Cole). By around two o'clock the auctioneers started selling horses and now came the interesting part. Soon after I noticed my little boy was nowhere to be found. I just wasn't paying attention and he had wandered off. It was a big place and lots of people around. I finally caught up with him playing in the dirt with another kid. Just then along came this gent looking for that kid. That's exactly when I first met Albert.

He said this is my grandson, Joe's boy. Now Joe, if you don't know, is a four-time Canadian calf roping champ, several time world qualifier, Calgary Stampede winner and hall of fame cowboy on both sides of the border. Joe is a little younger than me, but I've followed his career all my life. Albert and I hit it off right from the beginning. He and his bride Dorothy were true pioneers and carved a very successful ranch out of the foothills of the Rocky Mountains the old fashioned way – they both worked like hell!

Now hard work is not one of my favourite things, but I do have three passions: rodeo, playing pranks on little kids, and hunting.

The hunting one was just wishful thinking as I'd never shot anything in my life. Myself and my brothers would scare the hell out of a few Saskatchewan gophers from time to time, but that was about it. The only gun we had was a two-man single shot .22 caliber rifle. Do I need to repeat that? The ole gun was so worn out that when you cocked the hammer and pulled the trigger the spring was too weak to fire the bullet. So what you had to do was "load it, cock it and then say hit" and your brother would hit it with a hammer to fire the shell! I'm certain those gophers were laughing and saying here come those Nutting brothers and start making faces at us.

Albert and Joe were the real deal. Excellent horsemen, hunters, and outdoors men. Albert was telling of past experiences at Panther River, Ya Ha Tinda and Lost Guide Lake. Encounters with grizzly bear, big horn sheep and elk! This was absolutely thrilling to me and I couldn't wait to expose this sort of adventurous life to my sons. There was just one small problem: I didn't know a damned thing about it, I was as green as grass and scared of heights to boot. There was a little sport made of it from time to time too! Albert still calls me a gopher choker! I did have one thing going for me. I was a horseman; I'll give myself that much. And let me tell you, there are a lot out there that ain't. Including a big bunch of so-called instructors preaching horsemanship. My brag is this: Of all the kids, and there were many, that went on all the horse trips they were never hurt or injured or put in danger in anyway. They were looked after.

The first time I went up in the mountains was with Joe, Albert, and a guy named Jimmy. I remember Jimmy was well-mounted on a fast walking horse – good for him but it made the other guys have to trot. We went up to Kananaskis Country, riding up a power line, and made camp in the timber. Albert had a grouchy old roan mare for a pack horse and that night he tied her to a tree, hobbled her, built a little makeshift coral around her and put a bell on her. "She should be there when I need her in the morning!"

The next morning, Joe and Jimmy went one way and Albert and I went the other. It was big medicine for me! My first time in the mountains elk hunting. We rode up a mountain and down and up another one. Now my ass is dragging. Albert is several years my senior and he is doing fine. Tough as hell. We finally get to a good lookout, dismount and tie the horses up. It's a beautiful warm sunny fall day, the bugs are gone by now and the fall colors on the leaves are simply beautiful.

Albert gets comfortable and is glassing the other mountainside. I'm thinking, "If you shoot something over there who the heck is going to get it?" Shortly after I see he is enjoying a siesta in the sun. I was way too nervous for that.

It was finally time to head back to camp. It was just starting to fog in and pretty soon you couldn't see very far. I soon realized that any time you head to the hills you better be prepared for anything. I was pretty worried about getting lost and at that time I can remember looking at Albert's backside and thinking, "Don't die you old bugger, I'll never find my way out of here." And judging by the looks of him I could boil him for a week and he'd still be way too damn tough to eat. And with those humble first thoughts a great friendship was formed that remains intact to this day.

We rode for a couple hours and the fog got thicker. Finally, we were in camp before we even saw camp. Quite an experience for me and also quite a relief. That was a great introduction to what would prove to be a way of life for me and my sons.

Several years ago Albert got prostate cancer. He had to have an operation. I was pretty worried but underestimated just how tough an ole bird he is. He didn't even miss hunting camp. He didn't ride a horse that year for obvious reasons but looked after camp.

I went to visit him in the hospital but before I left I brought two magazines, a Western Horseman and a Playboy. I very carefully switched the covers and did a good job of gluing the cover of the Western Horseman to the Playboy. Albert was still pretty laid up and I put the magazines down out of Albert's reach. I wanted him to discover them on his own. He did a day or two later – I would like to have been a fly on the wall when he got things figured out. That little prank cheered him right up!

Campfire Memories

This was the start of our hunting adventures. My boys took to this like ducks to water. Back then I was doing well financially and would always ask the boys: would you guys like a trip to Disneyland or would you like to go to the hills? We have never been to Disneyland. One particular time we were in a camp that Albert called Poacher's Camp because you couldn't see the tent from the trail. We had spent the day riding and were coming down the mountain when we spotted a moose antler shed, then another, then six or seven, and then Alberta spotted an old moose carcass. Now even my young sons knew that this is a very dangerous situation because usually a bear owns that kill and will be very territorial about it. Albert had a gun, so did my oldest boy and so did I. So we sent my son Ben in there to get the skull and antlers. He was as scared as could be thinking a grizzly bear would show up to chase him off. He yanked the skull from the carcass and ran like hell. We got back to camp with our moose pans and skull, got supper done and Ben is still sulking. "That was a damn foolish thing you made me do today, Dad." Of course the kid was right, but it *was* exciting. Albert said, "You boys worry about bears too much, all you gotta do is put a hole in 'em, that changes their minds. Besides, a bear would have no interest in an old guy like me. But he might like you, Dallas, he might reach under the tent flap and pull you out." Dallas was just a little guy and knew he was getting teased, but he slept right under my arm that night. Those are campfire memories!

Now, more on getting early in camp. It's usually not a problem unless the "safety meeting" the night before went on too long, but a guarantee for getting up early is to use an "Indian alarm clock." The story here is that if the Indians wanted to get up early for battle, the night before they would drink six or eight cups of water before they went to bed. Now that will get you up early, or at the very least make you wish you hadda!

There's one thing old friends will do, everyone actually, but I probably am guiltier of this than most, is repeat myself, but I have to pass on a tale that Albert asks to hear every year in hunting camp: "The Story of the Ventriloquist and the Indians."

A ventriloquist was riding across the west and night was falling. An Indian camp was nearby and the ventriloquist thought he would enjoy their hospitality and maybe have a little fun at their expense.

He was treated very well, fed, watered and had a place of honor near the night's campfire. "Is that your horse, chief?" he asked.

C: "My horse."

V: "Can your horse talk?"

C: "Horse no talk."

V: "Is that so horse, you can't talk?"

The horse replied, "Yes, I can talk, it's just that no one here cares to hear what I have to say."

The chief was beside himself. The ventriloquist pressed on. "How are you treated here?" The horse replied, "Not so well of late. When I was young and fast it was fine but now I am old and slow and the chief hits me with his whip."

The chief was losing face here and was embarrassed. The ventriloquist then asked, "Is that your dog, chief?"

C: "My dog."

V: "Does your dog talk?"

C: "Dog no talk."

V: "Is that so, dog, you can't talk?"

The dog replied, "Oh, I can talk, it's just that no one here wants to listen to what I have to say." The chief is beside himself again. The ventriloquist presses on. "How are you treated here?" The dog replied, "Well not so good of late. Now I am older and can't catch the rabbits, the chief doesn't let me close to the fire."

The chief lost a lot of face and was embarrassed.

Then the ventriloquist asked, "Chief, is that your sheep?" The chief replied "SHEEP LIE!"

While I'm at it I'd better get another sheep story out of the way. This actually happened many moons ago at the Calgary Stampede.

My son Carson and I joined Albert and Dorothy at the Stampede to watch Joe compete in the calf roping. Back then there was a livestock show, horses, cows, sheep, etc. We were touring the barns when ahead of us was a cute little girl dragging her sheep, who was skidding on all four legs, across the alleyway. I went to help that kid and grabbed that sheep by the hind end and pushed it across the alley…. HONEST! Albert said, "I wish I had a camera – anytime I needed 20 bucks I'd just reach for that picture." He's never let that go – he chalked my actions up to "force of habit."

Another story he has on me is this. We were up in the Ya Ha Tinda in our tent listening to the elk bugle. That is very likely my favorite experience. Had a nice fire in the stove and a lantern glowing; we were right in the middle of what I call a "safety meeting" enjoying a cup of whiskey.

Just then an old motor home showed up and music started blaring (not really) but it took away the sound of the elk. It was the Water Valley Saloon Girls.

I said to Albert and Dorothy, "We can't put up with this, I better go over to their campsite and see if I can't quiet 'em down some. Turned out to be a lot bigger job that I thought. Took me danged near all night to get 'em to quiet down. I came back to camp rip-roarin' drunk and managed to get in my sleeping bag – trouble was I was nose to nose with their old dog Sadie! I would snore and Sadie would growl back. I woke up that morning after a good night's sleep not quite fresh as a daisy, but Albert and Dorothy looked a little frazzled! There were so many fantastic memories made over the years, some good and some really good.

The road up to the Ya Ha Tinda campground can get pretty treacherous. At the tail end of one season my son's plan was to head up to our camp, which was still up, shoot a sheep and have it ready when Albert and I got there to take the camp down. What really happened was this: he missed going around the last icy bend in the road and slid the truck and trailer down the mountain. The trailer broke off and rolled on its side with two horses in it. They got skinned up a bit but turned out fine. I was down below in town and it was a snowy, stormy night and I had no idea what had happened. My son had my truck and some other hunters pulled him back on the road and he managed to drive back to my house. A friend and I were out having a beer, and when we drove home, there's my truck in the driveway. I'm thinking great, we'll have a good visit and go get the camp out in the morning. On closer inspection my truck was a wreck. It was white four-door F150. A tree had gone through the back seat, the back panel was ripped off, there were kinks and bruises everywhere. I feared for my sons' health until I saw him standing in the living room through the window. I was so relieved I got the giggles! I got a hold of myself and thought, "Well I should at the very least give him hell for wrecking my truck!" But it just wasn't in me, plus he already felt bad enough on his own. I actually had to tell him it wasn't that bad – that truck is just iron – I can replace it. Then I started to tell him of all the trucks that my brothers and I had wrecked on our dad – but that would fill another book!

I'll tell a little story on Albert that I like. If you recall, we would head up to Pierce Lake every summer right after school was out. The timing on this is important as the fish are really biting that time of the year but tail off a bit as the season progresses. Albert and Dorothy and a grandson of theirs joined us this year but we went up a few weeks later and the usual fantastic fishing was not anywhere near as good. In fact, it was downright pitiful! In fact, Albert only caught one fish – and he was beginning to doubt all my earlier stories on fishing. He later said, "You know that one fish likely cost me $1000?" I replied, "Albert, you shouldn't complain – you coulda caught three!" The trip was not a loss, though. They have a beautiful golf course up there, and Albert accuses me of putting a ball deep in the woods – I say it was him. That particular year was fantastic for Saskatoon berries. Albert and Dorothy are two of the only people I know who pack bags in their golf bag for berries or mushrooms or whatever. Anyway, that was the end of golfing for that day as we headed home with a few gallons of berries.

Every fall found me and my boys up in the mountains with the Lucas crew. One particular hunt stood out in that it was cold, below minus 30 degrees. Now Albert and I were in our main camp down below but Joe, Lyle and Carson were up top with just what they had in their saddle bags and back packs, deep snow too. I'd be lying if I told you we weren't a little worried. Now it's -30 and we are in a canvas tent but we are snug as bugs. Lots of wood, lots of good grub and a good supply of whiskey. All we had to do was start the trucks every three or four hours. I forgot to mention that there were others worrying for those guys too – I guess there was some talk of getting a helicopter. They came down the next day. No sheep, though – no one worked harder for one either.

Alright, I got another joke for ya, this one is also an annual, as Albert requests it every year, usually the first night in camp. This joke is unique to me – remember I told you I have 10 brothers.

Well, I head to the rodeo, get on my bronc and get the living daylights stomped out of me, ending up getting my pecker stomped off. I end up in the hospital and the doc says, "Well, if you have a family member willing to donate we can build ya a new one." "That sounds pretty good, Doc, as I have plenty of family. I get the operation and a year goes by and I'm back for my check-up.

"How's your new unit workin' out for you?"

"Well, not bad, Doc, she's sure a beauty, I got one small complaint though!"

"What's that?"

"Why did you have to put Grampa's part in the middle?"

Albert always feigns indignation and says, "Why do you always look at me when you say that last part?"

One time up there, Albert shot a six-point elk right at daybreak. Joe was with him and was riding his mule. Joe has chaps made out of black bear hide and watching him come out of the timber wearing them he's lucky he don't get shot. They field-dressed this elk and right around the time I show up Joe hooks onto the elk and starts dragging him to the truck. He only goes so far and then the mule starts coming unglued so it takes five or six pulls with the mule trying to unload the elk. But the job gets done – there was a bit of a cut bank and Joe drags that elk right in the trailer. The jungle drums must have started to beat because when we got back to camp two of Albert's good old friends showed up and they have a jug of aiming fluid (most people call it whiskey) with them. I had the job of splitting that elk but I had three of the best consultants in the business in my corner. I got a picture of them. That was one happy day in camp.

One of those friends was Charlie. I mentioned him in the introduction. Charlie may be the best outdoorsman I know. As for putting up a tent that would still be up for you in a blizzard, or having the right kind of wood, and always prepared for any situation, he was the guy you wanted – in addition to which he was a hell of a cook. A guy showed me how to take a coffee can of sawdust and pour diesel fuel in it to use for fire starter. It's a real handy trick, so I showed Albert, but Albert said, "Don't let Charlie see you doing that." Charlie was all "old school". He showed us a better way by making fire sticks – just shaving wood chips from kindling, which makes a fire right away. Charlie is one of those guys who is a pleasure to have in camp – handy as hell and great company when the fire's getting low.

The other ole timer up there was Everett Ball, another real character. Everett knows and can sing every Wilf Carter tune there is and will sing them with little to no encouragement. He also knows every old joke in the world. Everett had a son named Doan and on one wintery occasion Albert hit the ditch and got his truck stuck in the snow. Shortly after, along came Everett and Doan and hooked on to the truck and got Albert out. Now whenever Albert recollects that story it goes like this: "I got stuck in a snow bank and got pulled out by the Balls!"

I gotta mention another time we headed out early. Joe was riding an Appaloosa gelding and that horse started getting waspy. He bucked and kicked halfway up the mountain and when he'd weaken a bit Joe would school him. This went on for quite a while. I've seen some good bronc rides in my time and this was sure one of 'em. Made me wonder about Joe's choice of events – I believe he could have made it to the pay window bronc riding too.

Bad Billy

I gotta tell ya about one of my customers when I ran the Imperial Oil bulk fuel station in Caroline, Alberta. This ole rancher's name is Merv. When I took over the business there was over $300,000 on the ledger. The way this works is my customers owe me that and I owe Imperial Oil that! That was about three hundred thousand more than my customers owed me at my last bulk station up north in Buffalo Narrows. The way it worked up there was you give me money and I give you fuel – in that order. Let me tell you I was more than a little nervous carrying that much debt.

Now my business office was also a bit of a gathering place for the ranchers. Fresh coffee and a place to visit your neighbors. They would also give me the gears every time fuel went up in price – you could say I was on the front lines. Merv reminded me the last time I saw him that I was never too sympathetic – I would tell those boys, "Fellows, you're safe dealing with me – I believe you can shear a sheep many times but you can only skin him once!" That would rile them up some. I even had a miniature violin and a cute little case. If they started getting too sad I would bring it down from the shelf and pretend to play it. Looking back I'm kinda surprised someone didn't break it over my head.

Merv had over a hundred head of cattle and half as many horses. I told him one time just sell one cow a day, you will be rolling in money. He replied, "What happens when I'm out of cows??"

"Well you're on your own then, partner!"

Now on to something that I think is pretty interesting. Shortly after Christmas, Merv was in the Longbranch Saloon. I joined him and asked, "How was Christmas?" Merv told me he spent it in Olympia, Washington visiting his mom and family. I said that sounds like fun – did all your family make it home?

Merv said, "Everyone but Bad Billy." Well every family seems to have one of these, but Merv's "Bad Billy" is better known as Dan or D.B. Cooper – that's right, the guy accused of hi-jacking a 727 airliner in 1971. If you need refreshing on this, D.B. Cooper hi-jacked and got a ransom of $200,000 and then parachuted out the back of the plane in the dark somewhere over Washington state, starting one of the biggest mysteries on the continent.

Merv's family moved to Caroline when Merv was young. When I met him he had a family of his own and had carved out a pretty good life for himself and family in the Caroline area with some good land and livestock purchases.

Merv would mention that he was a "catch colt" – that's an old ranchers' term for a colt that you are not sure of the sire, a fairly common occurrence on the range – and common enough in other situations too!

Merv's family moved on to Olympia but Merv stayed behind and moved in at a tender age with the Allstott family, who raised him. His brother Billy went on to join the army, get his pilot's license and take parachute training. They made a movie of his heist, "The Pursuit of D.B. Cooper," but no one ever could answer just who D.B. was. Billy would drop back in Caroline every now and again, never staying long – he even crashed a light plane in the pasture one time. His visits got less and less frequent and no one has heard hide nor hair of him for years. So now you know just part of the puzzle of D.B. Cooper!

So I Was Hired to be Buffalo Bill <u>Twice</u>

My brother Tony and I were flying down to New Orleans to see Mom and Dad and my brother and his family. He had a newspaper clipping saying they were going to start Buffalo Bill's Wild West Show at Eurodisney in Paris, France. They needed Buffalo Bill, Sitting Bull, Annie Oakley and a cast of cowboys and Indians. They were going to hold auditions at the Pawnee Complex in Hobbema in January. Tony said that I should try out.

I show up late and the place is a zoo. I gotta park way at the back of this field and the complex was full. I had an advantage as a friend of mine was working there and he told me, "Don't wait in any lines – just go find Jean-Phillipe and tell him I sent you."

I finally find Jean-Phillipe and tell him I'm here to hire on as Buffalo Bill. He says you're too late – we are already on our short list of B.B's. I said wait a minute, I told my buddy I couldn't make it till now and he said I would still get a shot – besides, I was beyond doubt the exact guy you were lookin' for.

That got him and he said OK, jump on that horse there. What I didn't know was this ornery white horse had been bucking the B.B. tryouts off earlier. I start walking up to the horse and a gal came running up: "Wait, wait, you have to sign your accident release form first." Say what now? Oh well I never thought about getting bucked off – but what the heck, not like it's never happened before!

Well, Ole Whitey started humping up and I pulled his head up (this was bareback) and dug him in the ribs. I kept him collected up and he started a little humpy but I got by on him and then Phillipe says lope him out in a figure 8. I did and he's really impressed. I thought, "What?" This was nothing special – that level of riding is pretty normal in Alberta.

Then he gave me the "Introduction script" and said learn that and then perform it to the crowd. I was not expecting this – I thought all I had to do was an interview in which I would tell him he was a fool if he didn't pick me.

There was one more B.B – most of these guys were just actors dressed up like B.B. out of Calgary and couldn't ride. This guy couldn't even get on the horse so I went over and boosted him on. Some dirty looks for that – I guess he was supposed to get on by himself. Well he was on, but kinda in the backseat of Ole Whitey. He kicked Whitey in the flank and Whitey spudded him right on his head.

Back to performing the opening act. I just pretended my little boys were in the stands and how much fun they would think it was. So I got on Ole Whitey and belted out the introduction lines.

Jean-Phillipe came over with a contract and I took it and said I would go over it. What happened next was another experience I was not expecting and was totally unprepared for. Paparazzi. Three newspaper reporters were asking me questions and of course it all was in the next days' papers – I snuck off to do this and really didn't want anyone who knew me to find out.

I wasn't too long out of the Indian reserve and was still pretty barky. CBC News radio interviewed me – ever been interviewed by surprise and no preparation? Me neither! I have it on tape but here is how some of it went:

CBC: It looks like they want to sign you up to a contract. Do you think you have what it takes to perform B.B.?

Ernie: Well, let's walk through this – I gotta ride around a bit, shoot off some guns and whoop it up with a bunch of Indians – I don't see my lifestyle changing much.

CBC: You obviously have some cowboy skills it will require.

Ernie: Well by the time I was 10 I was a cowboy. By the time I was 12 I was a Mountain Man. By the time I was 14 I was mountin' women.

What the heck was I thinking? It all went out on the air. At the time I had four little boys in every organized sport there was plus hunting plus rodeo, I was farming in Saskatchewan, I had a ranch where I bred, raised and broke and marketed world-class quarter-horses, I had an Imperial Oil bulk station and had just retrofitted our building and was president of the Longbranch Saloon. In other words, I was busy. I did the audition for fun, and it *was* fun. I really hadn't expected them to hire me. So I turned them down.

Several years later, I'm walking out of a restaurant in the morning when my cell rings. Here is a girl with a worse French accent than mine, asking me to meet in Ponoka for another audition. I'm wondering who is yanking my chain. Turns out it's the real deal. So I go up to Ponoka and go through the whole set up, and the Disney team asks if I'll meet with them again on the Sarcee Reserve. I audition and they say, "We want you, but we want you to be better." The girl gives me a DVD of the show and the script and tells me to make a DVD of my own and send it in.

After a couple of weeks, I email her back and say, "I'm ready to get on the plane, send me a 1st class ticket."

She emails back, "Wait a minute, we told you what to do: learn the script and make a DVD." Basically saying: "Don't wish your way here, earn it!"

So how the heck do you do that? The show is two hours long, 13 acts, B.B. stars in 10 of 'em. So I'm sitting up late one night watching David Letterman and pondering my situation. After 30 years Letterman still uses cue cards. So I made up a cue card summary of Act One – and went over it again and again. Then Act Two and so on and so on.

Now to make a video. I hired a professional who makes advertisements and promotional videos. Then I rented an arena and the cameraman, my faithful steed Bud and I made a video – actually a pretty dern good one if I do say so myself. We edited it and sent it off.

Now the deal with the show is if they got enough B.B.'s (I think they need three or four) they do two shows a night. When they need someone to fill the spot in the rotation you get the call. Well wouldn't you know it, I was offered a great position in Texas – just what I needed. It was a great opportunity and a brand new adventure. Six weeks into the job, the BBWWS calls again – there is a spot open – would I go to Paris? Well, boys, I had to turn them down – I was not going to trade what I had going on in Texas for Paris. But I don't know – maybe this story is not yet over.

So I Met Harv

We moved out of Buffalo Narrows in 1990. I moved north with a bride and a dog. I moved out seven-plus years later with the same bride, four little boys ages two, four, five and six (the dog died, had a private service for him and buried him up there on Nugget Island).

I bought a small ranch and started living the dream. My purchase was right beside what would turn out to be one of my very best friends. He had a rodeo ranch and took his bulls and broncs to professional rodeos. Well I was in heaven, building my own quarter horse ranch, raising, training and showing world class quarter horses and raising my boys. But I was very easily drawn away to the "thrills and spills and hospital bills" of rodeo. I loved helping my neighbor Harv gather and load and haul all his stock to the rodeo. Believe me, that is where the real rodeo is – getting those critters out of the bush pasture and on to a semi.

Now Harv and I had several things in common. We had the same sense of humor, meaning we both understood comedy and tragedy: to explain it further, if Harv got mowed down by a bull, why that's comedy; if it happened to me – that's tragedy. We shared the same vices, plus we even shared the same birthday – July 18, plus we both suspected the other of being a little dense.

Vegas

Harv would take rodeo stock down to Vegas for the finals. For those of you who don't know rodeo, the bulls and broncs get to Vegas the same way the cowboys do – they win their way there (actually the cowboys nominate and vote 'em there).

I flew down and joined Harv and drove back with him to the cattle liner with the stock. No, that sounds wrong – I got to ride up in the cab. But this all comes to bear later as I only packed for inside work. If you know me there is nothing I don't like about rodeo – the NFR, Thomas and Mac Arena are my cathedrals and the cowboys are disciples. It didn't take me long to make friends and I am still friends with most of them to this day. There was just one problem: I never slept at the time and was running on empty. At the rodeo performance the doggers started bronc riding and the bronc rider started calf roping – what was happening was I was taking very long blinks and missing a bunch of the rodeo.

One night Harv and I were gambling and doing very well – we could hardly see each other for the stacks of chips in front of us. By morning we could see each other very well. The house had broke both of us. The dealer was kind-hearted enough to give us each a chip for free breakfast, so off we went and ordered steak and eggs. As we were waiting Harv fell asleep. Our order came and I could not wake Harv. I ate my breakfast – still could not wake Harv – so I forked over Harv's steak and ate it too. Wouldn't you know it, just as I was finishing Harvs' steak he woke up. "I thought I ordered steak with this?!!" I muttered something like, "I dunno, Harv," and left. That's between him and the waitress now. No need me complicating things!

The rodeo ended and we are loading stock in the dark as usual and this fellow came up and said, "I bought a plastic horse (the life-size ones you see outside of western stores) and I wonder if you could haul it up to Calgary for me?" Harv said, "Do you know this guy?" I did – he was John Rudiger, a very well-known and successful Charlois cattle breeder who lived on Old Banff Coach Road west of Calgary. I said this guy is OK and we loaded the plastic horse in the back of the liner. John said, "What will you charge me?" Harv answered, "Same as another horse."

I have to mention the Small family. Butch Small, 12 time national finalist, and his rodeo family have a ranch in Dubois, Idaho. They have the pens set up so all – and I mean all – the Canadian stock contractors can come in and unload the stock. The feed and water are already set up for us. I never saw the ranch cause we always unloaded and loaded in the dark. I do want to mention that we had the best breakfast I've ever had courtesy of Butch's mom, brother Kevin and the rest of 'em.

They also put Harv and me up in Butch's log cabin, which was also his trophy room. Butch had quite a successful career. Now southeast Idaho in December can be a little chilly and this year did not disappoint. It was cold as hell. We got a little fire going in the cabin and if you recall earlier, I did not pack for this but Harv did. So I borrowed a pair of long underwear from him (I later wrapped 'em up and gave 'em back to him for Christmas – it was just something we fell into, exchanging x-mas gifts – more on that later).

The fire started roaring and it was getting pretty cozy so out came the whiskey and we had a pretty long and enjoyable safety meeting. Now I better mention there was only one double bed. We finally hit the hay. The long Idaho winter night came and went and the fire had long since gone out, leaving the cabin at a brisk 10 below. Harv and I woke up like a pair of spoons in a drawer. Uncomfortable.

We hit the trail, not missing too many saloons along the way, getting closer to the border. An evil thought crossed my mind when the border came in sight! "Say Harv, you don't suppose there is anything in that plastic horse, do you?"

It coulda been half full of cocaine and we would have been the perfect mules.

Bit of a Bump

As you can imagine with a pair like us, there were a few speed bumps on the road. Harv had a Bull Riders Only event down by Bragg Creek. It was quite entertaining – they even had a guy with a lit-up suit like the one in Electric Horseman. I used my big red horse to get the bulls out of the arena after they bucked. The night went well and there was a dance afterward. Harv and I drank our share and then slept for a while in the semi. It was the dead of winter but really toasty in the cab and we both went to sleep. Unbeknownst to me, Harv woke up and decided to practice his drunk driving.

When I woke up we were jack-knifed in the ditch with snow right up to the windshield and I don't feel well. I'm really disoriented and the semi is rocking with bulls in the back scrambling to get to their feet. My horse is back there too. Harv is slumped over the steering wheel and looks like he could be dead. He finally comes around and we start figuring out our plight. And it ain't good. It was two in the morning and the bar in town was emptying out. These guys took us to a neighbor to get his tractor to pull us out. We got to Louis' (he is the dad to a friend of mine) and told him our predicament. Louis looked at me and said, "Is that you, Nutting, you don't look so good!" I said, "Well now, Louis, you're not that good a looker yourself!"

Louis said, "Seriously, you look really bad, come in here." I had hit my face on the dash, smashed my two front teeth out and split my top lip open right up to my nose, and at that time I sported a big hairy blonde mustache.

I looked in the mirror but what I saw was not me. It looked like I had two big hairy bloody sausages on my face! One of the guys that drove us there offered to take me to the hospital in Rocky Mountain House. Now I really did look a mess but did not feel that bad – yet. The nurse was a bit shocked (I'm certain she'd seen worse) and did her best. She phoned the doc on call, explained the situation and he said he'd get there when he got there. You get no respect (nor likely deserve any) when you show up at a hospital in the middle of the night with alcohol on your breath. I said to the nurse, "Hand me the phone." Real bad idea. I told the guy to get in here as I had plenty of business for him – that started us out on the right foot. Not!

I waited and waited – you know, on the comfortable little bench with the paper sheet. Next thing I'm fast asleep, but when I wake up here's this guy sewing up my top lip! I don't know what hurt more, the needle and thread or the sound it made! I'm wiggling a bit and he said, "Stay still, I thought you cowboys were supposed to be tough." I thought, ok you, you jerk, sew away! Boy, it was all I could do to stay still with him working on me!

He got done and said, "You don't feel too bad yet but when the whiskey wears off you are gonna, here are some pills." I took his hand and put the pills in it. "Us cowboys are tough, give those pills to someone who ain't."

Four hours later I woulda pushed my grandmother down a set of stairs for those pills.

My good Samaritan buddy stuck with me and was driving me back from the hospital. I got to thinking and told him to swing by Harv's. The rig didn't look that bad and I looked in the passenger side and there were my two front teeth. I scooped 'em up and put 'em in my pocket. They are still in my roll-top desk.

The next morning, it was a Saturday, I gotta go to work. I had a fuel, fertilizer and oil business and was too cheap to do overtime. I had pipeliners coming in for fuel. Boy oh boy, talk about a long day. I could feel every beat of my heart in my face. And it would be worse when I got home. Harv came slinking in later in the day, told me my horse was fine – and I was fired! Again. We had as many friends as a wet dog after that one.

Now I did what I always do when I really screw up – I hid out for a while. I finally showed up at my saloon for lunch. There was a few of my buddies just waiting for me after hearing all these rumors. One of the guys said, "I heard you and Harv screwed up again."

Me: "Nope, you heard wrong."

Him: "I heard you put the semi in the ditch and you lost your teeth."

Me: "Nope, you heard wrong."

Him: "I'll bet you lunch that I'm right."

I reached in my pocket, put my two front teeth on the table.

Me: "Didn't lose my teeth, here they are – I'll have the thoup."

A little later, I went to the dentist to get fitted for a bridge. He put in a plastic one while he built the permanent one. He told me not to play around with it as they aren't built too rugged.

Later that night I'm down in the barn forking horse manure and I'm fooling around with my plastic teeth and I break 'em. But not right out, just on one side – so it's like a swinging gate. SHIT, this is horrible. I whisper to my oldest son, "Come up to the house and help me glue my teeth." He runs away – that's spooky stuff to a seven-year old. I'm on my own.

I head up to the house thinking about my task.

Job One: Do not glue your lip to your teeth. I got all lined up and put Kleenex between my teeth and my lip. I hold my teeth in place with my fingers. I get the Krazy Glue out and "gink, gink," glue 'em up! Well wouldn't you know it, I glued my damn finger to the inside of my teeth. I had to cut my finger off my teeth with my Leatherman.

Back to the drawing board.

"Job Two: Do not glue your lip to your teeth – or your fingers!"

I get 'er all lined up again, this time keeping my finger out of it. I hold the plastic teeth in place with my tongue. Gink, gink, got 'em glued up. Yep, you guessed it. I glued my damn tongue to the inside of my teeth. Well I tried cutting my tongue free but had to weaken – hurt like hell and blood everywhere. I was whipped! I turned on the TV and comforted myself with the thought "It's not gonna be stuck there this time next year."

The kids started coming in, it's getting near bed time and I am still far from getting out of the dog house. So I'm trying to pretend there is nothing amiss.

Now, for those very select few who have ever glued their tongue to their teeth, you will know exactly what I'm talking about. You look exactly like you glued your tongue to your teeth – you simply cannot fake otherwise.

After listening, at length, to what a dumbass I was, I finally went to the bathroom, got my knife out and did it like you would taking off a band aid. YAHOOOO!

Mutual Friends – Ernie and Ernie

Through Harv I met a guy who was unique in a way that touched everyone he knew: my old friend Rodeo Hall of Famer for 2011, Ernie Marshal. He's not with us anymore. Rodeo announcer Dave Paulson officiated his funeral and I have to say he did a bang-up great job. There is not a rodeo clown working who did not include some of Ernie's material. His one act with a $10 bill and a fishing pole was priceless. He genuinely loved joking with the kids – and they genuinely loved Ernie back. I know – I had four little boys who adored him. He even had his own midway ride named after him!

Harv and I wanted to haul a load of cattle from Alberta to Saskatchewan. So I got 'em gathered before 10:00 am and Ernie showed up around 5:00 pm – that's working on "Harv time." "Where's Harv?" "I dunno – thought he was with you." It didn't take very long to figure out what the deal was. I was hauling cattle to our farm and Ernie was trading in an old "Pot" cattle liner for a newer "straight" liner.

Now ever since my altercation with waking up without my teeth I've had trouble sleeping in a moving vehicle. So while Ernie was driving I was awake and when it was my time at the wheel Ernie slept like a baby. Here is the time line. We loaded the cattle around 5:00 pm after I'd spent a full day rounding them up and other ranch things. We then drove through the night and unloaded the cattle at daybreak in Saskatoon and then headed on to Regina to switch trailers. We got that job done and now were "Alberta Bound." I still can hear Ernie saying to me, "Come on, get 'er in the big gear." You see, Ernie was an excellent "skinner," while I have always been cautious, to put it politely – others have said I drive like an old granny! We were getting near the Alta/Sask border and it's getting close to nightfall on our second day. This means we were also getting close to the weigh scales. Now, let me explain: at the weigh scales, weight is seldom the issue – permits, working condition, what you are hauling, etc, etc, are.

In our case, not all the lights were in working condition. So we decided to pull 'er over and go by 'em later in the night. Now, Ernie was a comedian even when he wasn't working. We pulled the rig over and were both gonna hit the sleeper. Ernie looked at me and said, "We can sleep pole to pole, or we can sleep hole to hole, but we can't sleep pole to hole." I laughed so much with that grinning little bugger – how the hell am I supposed to get to sleep now!

Ernie hauled stock to my home town rodeo at Sundre one year – and by the way, I always regretted we didn't hire him to work that rodeo. Anyway, I said, "Ernie, why don't you come and stay at my place, instead of in the sleeper in the rig?" Well a lot of years have gone by and my boys aren't little any more. They are all six footers – but Ernie is still 5'6" with his hands in the air.

My oldest son and Ernie bumped into each other going to the bathroom in the morning and my son said something that made me so proud of him. Ernie looked up at my boy and said, "I remember a time when you used to look up to me."

My son replied, "I'll always look up to you, Ernie."

The River Crossing

This is a story right out of the movies. It was a beautiful spring day in mid-June. The Clearwater River was flooding because of a combination of recent rains and the snow melt coming off the Rocky Mountains. The river jumped its banks and stranded about 30 head of Harv's rodeo cows and calves on a small island. Harv phones up and tells me to come over, he has a plan (when will I learn – I think I was a lot like my big red horse – he was really easy to catch because he was as interested as me as to what dumb thing was next).

Here's Harvs' plan. Harv, his son and I and would jump our horses in the river, swim to the island and force the head back to the mainland and grass. What could go wrong? We load our horses and head off. We get to our destination, unload, check our gear and head out. Now anyone who knows about fording a river – and there will be damn few of you – knows this: it's not about where you enter the river, it's all about where you can get out!

Harv's son jumped in, and it was a jump, about three feet off the bank. Then it was my turn. Now, neither I nor my horse had ever done anything near like this before. Well, no turning back now. My horse did everything ever asked of him, as any well-trained horse will do, but let me tell you in this day and age, there are damned few well-trained horses or horse people who even know how to get that job done. I gave Bud a kick and in we jumped. Harv brought up the rear. The river was only 20-25 yards wide but let me tell you, it was a rugged 25 yards. Cold and fast-moving and no real way to tell if a stump or a tree would come along and take you out. Now horses have a lot of traits like people. Some are brave, some are timid, some are smart and some make the smallest of tasks difficult. And some are strong swimmers and some are not. Harv's son's horse was not a strong swimmer.

That horse was struggling. Meanwhile I made the bank, and then Harv did too. Harvs' son was still not there and he was kinda up on his knees on the horse when they both went under! Harvs' son can't swim and came up with his arms up and shouted, "Harv!!" Harv threw his rope – and missed! I threw my rope – and snagged him! Now this is not a testament to our respective roping skills, as mine are average at best. This is just what happened. I pulled Harv's son out of the river and heard these words for the first and only time in my life: "Thanks for saving my life, Ernie."

We watched his horse tumble down the river – first his head and then his heels. That was a pretty sobering sight. While we were watching this, Harv's horse jumps in the river and goes home.

That horse wound up on the bank on the other side, safe and sound but spent. Here's our predicament: three cowboys and one saddle horse on the wrong side of the river. Harv comes up with a plan. (I know, I know.) He says, "I'll take your horse, gather the herd and we will force 'em in the river right here." Now some of you have been exposed to the rodeo bucking bulls and how cantankerous they can be. Well meet their mothers! They are downright waspy – they will chase you down a gopher hole. I never left a tree I couldn't climb.

Harv finally showed up and told us when he came upon the herd they all jumped in the river and headed home. All but three calves –we took my rubber raft over the next day and snared 'em and tied 'em up and got 'em back with their mommas the next day without incident.

You can see now we still have this one minor problem. A raging river between the three of us and our horse trailer. The plan was this. I would ride Bud and tow Harv and his son across. We had two lariats left as one was still on the first horse. If we had three we might have been able to span the river but I doubt it.

Bud was a powerful swimmer and in we jumped and I was dallied to the saddle horn. Then in jumped Harv and his son. Turns out we were asking too much of my horse and down the river we go. I remember shouting encouragement – come on, come on Bud – and he responded by trying harder. We made it to shore but there was no place to get out. Bud went over on his side – he was spent and resting and I was standing on his belly side still holding the dally. The other two swim to shore and I can still see them scrambling up the muddy bank like drowned rats.

We took a little time to catch our breath (not a lot) and then got ole Bud up – had to push him in the river to get him to a place he could get up the bank. Now Harv's son went to get his horse off the river. His horse was standing on a little shelf just big enough for his four feet down a 15 foot bank. He had to be pushed in the river too to get to a place we could get him out.

We took off most of our wet clothes and walked back to the trailer, leading two worn-out horses.

I can still picture Harv walking back with his hat, long underwear and boots all soaking wet. Now remember, this was mid-June. I always meant to ask him: "Are those long johns just finishing up last year's season or are they a fresh pair for the upcoming season?"

Story tellin'

Story tellin' is a great cowboy tradition. It ranks right up there with ridin' and ropin' cause there is also a lot of campfire sitting in a cowboy's life. Harv's campfire was a cattle liner and I was fortunate enough to travel many miles with him. Harv was always good company. He was one of those guys that could tell a great story or joke. Now everyone thinks they are that guy but very few really are. There is a real method to telling a joke – rhythm and timing and execution! I'll illustrate my point with this short story. By the way, there is a real talent to listening to one also!

Here goes. Men in prison have to while away the long hours of tedium and boredom. To do this they tell stories and jokes. Trouble is they've heard 'em all a thousand times. So to speed things up they've numbered the jokes. Things would get quiet and an inmate would shout out "Number 7" and get a roar of laughter. Then later on an inmate would shout out "Number 15"(a particularly funny one) and bring the house down. One day a newcomer, after learning the system, thought he'd try it himself and shouted out "Number 9." Nothing, not a peep! He asked his cellmate, "What the heck did I do wrong?" His cellmate replied, "Well nothing, it's just that some people don't know how to tell a joke."

Harv was not that guy. I'll tell you one of his favorites (and mine). This ole rancher was sending his son away to college – gave him 1000 bucks and put him on the train. The boy had never before enjoyed so much freedom and money and it wasn't long before he partied and drank and frittered away all the money (that ring any bells out there, parents??).

Now he knew his dad had one big weakness: his ole dog Blue. He loved that ole hound and would brag that ole Blue was very likely the smartest dog in the land. So the boy wrote home and told his dad of this professor who thought he could teach a dog to read if he had the right candidate – all he needed was a super smart dog and 1000 bucks

The rancher had Blue and the money on the next train. Well, same story – didn't take the son long to go through all those funds too. So, time to go to the well again.

This time the boy had to get a little more creative so he says to his dad, "You won't believe it, Blue picked up reading like a duck to water. The professor said he's never seen such a clever dog." This was music to the rancher's ears - he knew it all along.

The boy continued, "The professor thinks he can teach ole Blue to talk but it will take a little more cash, just another 1000 bucks." Now the rancher was never a rich man but this sounded like money well spent so off went the dough.

Now the semester has come and gone and it was time to come home. The rancher kept in touch with the boy on Blue's progress and it was better and better each time. They were to arrive on the train and the rancher had a crowd of well- wishers and a band on the train platform to welcome them back. This was gonna be a glorious occasion. The train arrived, the band started playing but no son and no Blue!

The train finally pulled out of the station and the band went home and the crowd dispersed. The rancher just sat there with his head in his hands.

Some time passed and down the tracks came the son. "Boy, what happened? Why weren't you on the train? Where's ole Blue??"

"Sit down dad, I got some bad news. Me and Blue were riding on the train comin' home to what we figured would be a hero's welcome. Blue was just sitting there reading the newspapers when he began talkin'!

"Blue talked of this and that and then he started talkin' about how he used to see you and the hired gal goin' out to the woodshed, just a carrying on! I couldn't believe my ears! I got to thinking if Ma got any wind of this why your life wouldn't be worth living. I finally had enough of Blue's lies and I took him and threw him on the tracks -killed him!

The ole rancher took his time digesting this then he spoke. "Are you sure that lying dog is dead?"

Pendleton Roundup

Now stock contractors get really cool jackets. I was always after Harv to give me one – he had 100 of 'em. I had a blood Bay quarter horse stud colt that was just what I was looking for – an outcross stallion and handsome as hell. There was just one problem – he was a real outlaw. He simply did not want to be a saddle horse. You could catch him and do his feet but when you saddled him he would buck and buck and not let the halter shank get tight. I told Harv of my troubles and he said: "Bring him over and we will take him to the Olds College rodeo practice night and try him out – see if he will buck!"

We put him in the chute and a college kid got on him and we opened the gate. That horse exploded out of there and sent that kid to the moon! I thought we might have to shoot him his lunch. The horse kept it up and soon the pro cowboys were winning day money, then rodeos on him. He earned his way to the Canadian Finals Rodeo and the National Finals Rodeo in Las Vegas that first year as a three year old, which is really young, horsewise, for that level of competition. Harv named him "Buffalo Narrows." There will be a few tough bare riders who still remember him.

Now I told Harv: you owe me one of those cool jackets. The next season I rode over to Harv's to help gather stock. It was a warm and sunny day when I started out. We got the stock gathered up and had a bit of a safety meeting. By the time we were ready to go home a bit of a storm had brewed up and I mentioned it again that it would sure be nice to have a jacket. Harv brought out an old battery-acid-eaten, oil-stained jacket that I wouldn't start a fire with. After careful deliberation I took that jacket to town to get it monogrammed. I asked the girls in the shop if they would be offended to do a very special job for me – and this was it: Big Time F@*#ing Stock Contractor. I even got them to put "Harv" on the sleeve. I wrapped it up and gave it to him for Christmas.

Now back to the Pendleton Roundup in Oregon. A town of 17,000 doubles for the September week. They use the entire infield as the arena, race track and all. The pick-up men have their job cut out – they use five of 'em at once. This

107

is authentic western, the home of the famous Pendleton Run. The timed-event cattle start out on the dead run. Great watching!

One night it rained hard on the grassy infield and six helicopter gunships from the military base came over and fanned the grass dry – that was worth the trip alone! In between the rodeo events they have Indian horse races on the track.

The parade is spectacular – no engines, everything is pulled by horse, mule or oxen. Also, every surviving Rodeo Queen rides in the parade, all wearing their original queen attire – absolutely beautiful, what wonderful ambassadors to the greatest sport in the world. Their outfits go back for display in the windows of the many shops in Pendleton ready for the next year.

They also have the most wonderful outdoor theater, Happy Canyon, that tells the tale of the wild west from the fighters and all. As a rodeo committee man myself, I really have to tip my hat to the Pendleton Stampede Committee for all your hard work. You guys are doin' it right!

Harv

I was offered a great opportunity in Texas. I told Harv as we were both at the Canadian Finals Rodeo. Also my mom was real sick and I was told she would not make the night (she didn't). I asked Harv if he would sit up with me and drink a little whiskey. Harv realized the severity and he and another old friend, Jack, sat up and helped me get through a tough ole situation. Through all my moves Harv was one of the very few people I would talk on the phone with once a week. Anyone that knows me knows I am not a phone talker. It stems from growing up in the country on a "party line," which means there are several families on one line – a rural thing. And with 15 people in the same house – well, you can see the situation. So now I simply do not feel comfortable visiting on a phone for long.

I was in Veal Station, Texas, north of Fort Worth, when Harv phones up and gives some bad news.

"They tell me the grim reaper's got me." Harv's words. Apparently they did some exploratory surgery and simply closed him up and sent him home. He had pancreatic cancer and it was the galloping kind. I didn't get to visit Harv too many times after that.

It was very obvious that Harv's time was close to up. But I never saw fear or anxiousness in him over meeting his maker. It wasn't arrogance, it was more like calmness, a kinda "I am what I am" thing. He lived his life rough, tough and hard to bluff, of that there was no doubt, but I also saw him give free passes to his rodeo to kids who had nothing but holes in their pockets.

I got to the hospital and Harv looked pretty damn frail. We started talking and the conversation went to bucking horses. He said something about some horse and I said, "I think the same." Harv said, "Don't you start agreeing with me now!" The last time I saw Harv I walked in the hospital and I was just standing there watching him sleeping. There was very little of him left now. He woke up and saw me and smiled. He held out his hand and I grabbed it and he said "Ernie." It was the first and only time he ever called me Ernie – it was always "Nut" or "Nutting." I held his hand and he closed his eyes. My good friend Harv left us right then and there.

And Now for the Rest of the Story
(with apologies to Paul Harvey)

One of the best trips I've ever had with my sons was when we drove down to Rancho Santa Margarita, California to visit my brother and his family. But this is just an intro to another story. This is about three brothers who lived right down the street from my brother. You know them but you won't know their names. Their names were McGonnigal – James and the twins, Jeffery and Joseph.

They may be the first guys who lost their jobs to animation. They were kind of quirky and the three brothers lived in a moderate home and had enough royalty money to keep them going comfortably. They had a pretty good gig in advertising but like I said got moved out. This is not a happy story as there was a home invasion in this quiet little neighborhood and they were robbed and murdered.

And now for the rest of the story. I will tell you their professional nicknames and you will know exactly who I'm talking about.

SNAP, CRACKLE & POP.

POLICE THINK IT IS THE WORK OF CEREAL KILLERS.

HAHAHAHA – Did I get ya? Come on tell the truth – did I?

Horse Training

This is something that is close to my heart. I loved horse training. As I said before, horses are as individual as people are. My son and I watched a TV show on how the British cops train their horses. Boy, was that ever impressive! At the end of it all this cop was on his horse and in front of them was a paper that looked like a brick wall. The cop asked the horse to jump through it and the horse did without hesitation! That told me that the horse had absolute trust in his rider and that whatever he was asked to do would not hurt him! That's a very important point because a bunch of trainers out there believe you gotta hurt 'em to get things done! Anyway, I said we gotta try that and did. It was mainly my son's doing. We started out with paper just chest high and worked our way up, culminating in my son leading the Vermilion College rodeo team into the arena by jumping through a paper wall with the university crest on it.

I would go to horse training clinics to better myself but the funny thing is the bigger bunch of them are tricksters. The biggest trickster of 'em all in my experience is a guy who calls himself the "Horse Whisperer" or the "guy who listens to horses." This guy is truly a case of the "Emperor having no clothes." He's just a huckster selling outdated ideas to gullible people who have zero experience but are desperate to get along with their horses. I went to his clinic and left half way through – got tired of his obvious crap.

I trained a young stallion to do tricks almost by accident. I went to catch him and he ran off, so I chased him and chased him, I would not let him rest. Finally I said, "Whoa." If he stopped, I let him rest – that's his reward; if he didn't I just chased him more. He got solid on "Whoa" very quickly and then I went on to walk, trot, lope, come when I whistled. He took to the training very well.

Now I'm going to tell you what every horseman knows, but they don't know that they know it. We have all seen a horse in the pasture when a fly lands on them – they wiggle their hide to get the fly off. Those are called "twitch muscles." But those muscles are just from the shoulders on back – not on the neck. When a fly lands on their neck they either shake their head from side to side or up and down depending where the fly landed. That's how you train a horse to say "yes and no" – just pinch your horse's neck till you get a response, then reward him with a pat. My stallion got solid on that in less than two days.

Now some of you have heard the old wives' tale of the guy who packed an alarm clock in his pack string. The alarm went off and the pack horse ran off bucking his pack off. I don't believe that story for a moment! The last thing you need in camp is an alarm clock, in fact you go to camp to get away from them!

I will tell you of a mistake I made riding in the Sundre Rodeo parade. I had my cell phone with me and I put it in my saddlebag and it was on vibrate. There were almost three calls that came in, unbeknownst to me, but here is my good ole big red horse going nuts. I couldn't figure it out! He must have thought I packed a rattlesnake. Live and learn.

A friend of mine named Jim down the road trained his horse to allow the dog to jump on with him. When the kids were small we would help Jim move his cows from pasture to pasture. This particular day we chased his cows to the home place and Jim was dyin' to show off this trick. He whistled for the dog and the dog jumped up and the horse bucked 'em both off. He was sittin' on the wrong horse! Sometime later we were sitting in the Longbranch Saloon and that story came up. I said to Jim, "I couldn't help but notice the dog got bucked off last!" That was a funny but a little unfair, since Jim was a pretty good bull rider in his day.

The Horse Ride

I always enjoyed taking horses from my ranch in Alberta out to the farm in Saskatchewan. My kids and their cousins loved going on horse rides and back in Saskatchewan you can ride for miles on dirt roads and never have to open a gate. Part of the fun was exploring old abandoned homesteads from pioneers and settlers long gone. This day contained two of my favorite things – giving kids horse rides and pulling tricks on them.

There were five kids and I – we were well mounted and well provisioned. We headed south towards the North Saskatchewan river. I started preluding the trick I planned on playing on them. I told them we could explore this old farm building, but had to be very careful about wild animals like badgers, coyotes and foxes that might have taken up residence there. So as we were checking out this particular homestead I tried to make it as spooky as I could, saying, "There's a badger – get back!" And so on.

As always, any time you explore these ole places you find neat old artifacts. My niece Lindsey found an old tobacco can rusted shut but something clunking around inside. I told her that old Ed Nelson used to keep his money in tobacco cans and that there could be thousands of dollars in it! There is nothing more – and I mean *nothing* – more exciting to a kid than finding treasure.

After planting that seed I started the conversation on how we were going to divide this up. Lindsey was in the camp that it was finder's keepers. I told her we were all on this expedition together and should come up with a fair solution. This conversation was going nowhere and no agreement in sight. I'll come back to this later.

We mounted back up and headed south again, finally coming to McRobbie's, another old homesteader's place, long, long since abandoned, on the banks of the mighty North Saskatchewan. There was a bit of a porch, a main room and a bedroom. You couldn't swing a cat in there. (Where on earth did that saying come from – I'm gonna look it up.)

My plan of course was to scare the kids. I opened the first door very carefully and looked in the tiny porch with extreme caution. Now the second door I was doing the same and my nephew Scott was crowding me trying to look over my shoulder. I stepped aside and pushed him in – scared the heck out of him! Now my next plan was to do exactly the same with the back bedroom, but the kids were wise to me now. So I figured I'd walk in there and jump back in fake terror.

What happened next pretty near scared me to death!

Inside the bedroom were two turkey vulture chicks about a foot and a half tall. When I walked in they spread their wings and hissed at me. I dang near had a heart attack! Scared the hell out of me!

I later told my dad of this and he drove down there. He poked his head in the window. Momma buzzard was home and flew out the window over my dad's head dang near giving him a heart attack.

We had our lunch and started heading back to the farm. There was a little dissension in the ranks in that Lindsey was the only one getting rich. On the way back our neighbor had a buffalo herd. As they were alongside the fence we dismounted and Lindsey was picking grass and feeding the buffalo calves through the page wire fence. Unbeknownst to me the boys opened the rusty old tobacco can (with 30-year-old dried-up tobacco in it – surprise, surprise) emptied out the contents and filled it back up with fresh buffalo shit. And put it back in her saddle bag.

We got back to the farm, got the horses put away and headed to the house for the discovery. Everyone is gathered round and we open the can. Poor Lindsey is pawing through this fresh buffalo shit looking for treasure. It finally dawns on her it ain't what she was hoping for. Other than that it was a pretty eventful day.

The Charity Benefit

A real tragedy happened to a gal in Caroline along this time. She was married to a guy with a little girl and was pregnant when her husband was killed in a vehicle accident coming home from work. Then her little daughter was diagnosed with cancer. Wow! Take a moment to think about that!

Well, not only did that mobilize a small community but the entire area. We put on a benefit auction like you have never seen. It was held in the ice rink and in the parking lot. The donations included chores, cows, chickens, ducks, hamsters, puppies, kittens, loads of gravel, drill stem pipe, furniture, sports equipment, pictures, etc. If I think of more contributions I will add them.

Four auctioneers donated their time. The items that could not be there physically were written on an 8½ x11 paper and taped to the wall. Things like three hours of welding; school kids donating yard work; groceries; plumbers and electricians donating their time to be auctioned to whomever needed their services.

At the time I had a pretty fancy stallion so I donated a stud fee, and I also had the fuel and fertilizer station, so I donated two tonnes of fertilizer. The place was abuzz with activity and as I was walking by five local married gals they said, "Ernie, what are you donating, you cheapskate?"

I replied, "I'm donating five dance lessons with me! Every ole hen in the county will want to dance with a handsome rooster like me!"

Guess what happened – they put a paper on the wall, "Five dance lessons with Ernie." The auctioneer came over and said, "Is this a joke?" No joke, the gals said – get going.

Well, the bid got to $300 and the auctioneer stopped again. Are you ladies kidding? No – keep going! These girls were using this opportunity to give their donation. The bidding stopped at a whopping $1900, and the girls wrote out their checks. The auctioneer asked, "Who is getting the dance lessons?" One of the gals announced, "It's for our husbands!"

A day later my dad phoned up from Mississippi and asked, "What the heck are you doing selling dance lessons?"

The end of the story is this: we raised just short of $40,000 – not bad for a small community. The lady's little daughter beat her cancer, she had a healthy baby girl, she went on to a successful career in real estate, and sometime later got into a great relationship. She is now a proud grandmother and last I heard everything was fine!

So I Built a Saloon

I came into town in 1990. Caroline is a small place of 400 or so. It never seems to grow. My old friend Albert said the reason for that is that every time a baby is born a guy leaves town – sometimes two!

There was an old barn on main street that was empty. They tried a few businesses in it but none stuck. There was talk of turning it into a western style saloon but it was just that – talk! But this was something that struck a chord in me so myself and eight other guys threw in $2000 each (I wanted everyone to put in $10,000 but that didn't happen) and we started the long journey from talk to actually selling whiskey! And believe me there are a lot of hoops to jump through. No bank would touch us because most bars go broke.

Now anyone who really knows me knows I hate politics and I especially hate politicians of all stripes. I hate the conservatives, can't stand the liberals, and think the socialists should be chased in the sea and shot! But right around this time there was a government committee formed to lend money to small ventures that couldn't get funding from normal sources. One of the partners in the saloon nominated me to be on the West Central Alberta development board. There were about 12 of us from small towns in central Alberta. What it really was a slush fund for party faithful. Surprise surprise! We borrowed roughly $200K and were in business. I do remember asking if this was ethical – me being on the board and getting a loan from the board. The head guy almost started giggling. So we signed the papers. There was a clause or two that came back to bite us, but more on that later.

Running a saloon may be one of the hardest things to manage there is. Lots of cash, liquor, long hours, etc. But here I am with eight partners all pulling in different directions. I can remember my grandfather Scott's voice ringing in my ears from when I was 10 years old; he said, "Remember this – a partnership is a poor ship to sail on." What the hell was he talking about?? I know now!

What an experience between the partners, the staff, the creditors and the clientele. The odd time I'd drink too much and ride my horse through the establishment! On one occasion I heard an old friend say, "Look at the two assholes on that horse!" We had a knife fight, a gun fight and one guy tried to burn us down.

Let's start with the knife fight. It wasn't much really. Some punk pulled a knife out and pointed it at our young bartender. My big Irish friend Roy got up, pushed the knife hand aside and punched that dummy right between the eyes! Apparently he went through the front door and lay crumpled up in the street. The police were called and got there a little later and the knife wielder was still incoherent. The police took a statement, looked around, saw that a bit of western justice had just been dished out, and left.

The gun fight wasn't much either. It was in the fall – hunting season, when lots of strangers are in the country. Wouldn't you know it – it all started around the pool table, which is where most bar fights originate. There was an argument and one fellow said, "I'm going to get my gun and settle this," and out he goes. The bar maid was looking out the window and hollered, "He's got a rifle." I wasn't there but apparently there were no heroes. The guy walked in to an empty saloon. There was one little old lady crouching behind the VLT machine she was playing – guess she figured it was about to pay off. Apparently the police caught up with that guy and this being Canada he probably had to promise not to be bad again and they would let him go.

The guy that tried to burn us down was the most serious. Ironically, it was on the day that we organized our "branding party." The saloon was rugged, western style, with plank walls, a long split timber running down one side to sit on, and a peanut barrel with the shells going on the floor. If you have been in a western bar you may have seen horse and cattle brands decorating the walls. In most cases drawn on or sometimes burned on a shingle and hung up. I did it a little different. The way we promoted this was for $10 you would get a steak, a glass of beer and you could put your branding iron in the fire outside and come in and put your brand anywhere but on the waitress! It worked out a lot better than what you think it might!

The party went on all afternoon and then we had a band playing to a full house. As it carried on it got rough and rowdy, as it should. But then the trouble started! A stranger came in and was acting an ass and our manager asked him to leave, so he pushed her and a local boy clocked this jerk! What happened next could have turned into a disaster.

This guy goes and gets a five-gallon jerry can full of gas and splashes it on the back wall and puts the can under where the natural gas fixture enters the building. Then he lights 'er up! We are full to capacity inside, band playing, dance floor right full. The manager comes and calm as a cucumber, whispers to me, "The place is on fire." Now I was in the saloon all afternoon drinking beer but when I saw the back wall in flame and flames shooting out of the mouth of the jerry can it sobered me up! I firstly held my hand over the jerry can and moved it away. The wall was aflame but so far just the gas was burning. I took the fire extinguisher and put it out. The band kept playing and no one missed a dance. Hardly anyone knew what happened. A few guys headed out to catch the bad guy – I hoped they didn't catch him because he deserved to be choked to death! I was worried about fire starting in behind the wall so I took the fire extinguisher in the basement, stuck it between the floorboards and gave her a big burst! The yellow powder came out upstairs right behind the drummer in the band.

So far no big harm done. The police were called and the fire department. Last call was called and the place emptied out! A local guy and myself stayed and told the police all we knew. Then the fire department guys showed up. Biggest fight of the night was me trying to stop those boys from stripping the outside boards off my saloon with those big axes. Where the hell do you get axes like that?

Everything calmed down and it was agreed that we should stay in there overnight in case the guy came back or the fire started up. So to keep us both occupied we each took turns being bartender and tried to have one drink out of every bottle in the joint. When the staff showed up for the next business day we were as pickled as two cowboys could get!

Now remember I mentioned getting financing from the government? There was a clause in there stating if we grossed more than such and such we had to pay them a royalty. Well we did that our first year but we also spent it all! They wanted us to dig up 10K out of our own private pockets on top of the loan and interest. I argued that the business couldn't afford it, that we upheld our responsibilities, new jobs, new business, etc. and were not in a position to pay extra. Wouldn't you know, this little government pissant got all important (wish I could remember his name) and it turned a little ugly. I said what if a third party sat in – whose side would they take? Say a third party like the local newspaper? I have never seen anyone cave in so completely. We were let out of our contract – by this time the bank was ready to take us on as we had a good year's track record under our belts and we put that chapter behind us.

Now, on to the staff. None of the partners wanted to manage the place themselves, but they didn't want any of the other guys to run the place either. Our first manager, well the job was just too much, he was in a little over his head. There was one bartender – every time he worked the day's take was down $100. He was stealing from us but nothing was gone! All the checks and balances worked out, I'm just short $100. I was very busy on all fronts at this time but I started putting more time checking in on the saloon. Finally, at shift change I come in and as he is putting on his coat an empty 40 oz. bottle of whiskey falls out. He picks it, up puts on his coat and heads out. I think nothing of it right then. The next morning I'm thinking of the situation and I gotcha! What this rascal was doing was sneaking his own bottle of whiskey in and selling it under my roof! That's why it was so hard to catch him – nothing was gone – he was simply stealing sales!

My new manager was Maggie. Hard working, honest as the day is long and just cantankerous enough to keep customers coming in and the business to work. She was exactly the right gal for the job. She organized trail rides, poker rallies, all kinds of things and generally kept the place hopping. We even started making money! The bankers warned me – as long as your partners are struggling, you will get along, as soon as you start making money you will start fighting! Boy was he right!

Maggie got everything on the right track and our menu was great – I would buy my son's 4-H beef and serve it in the saloon. Our lunch crowd would fill the place.

One of our daily lunch specials was "soup and a bun." We had a mother and daughter team working for us and the soup and the buns were homemade. My buddy and I came in for lunch one day and my friend said, "I'd like soup and a bun, but I'd like two buns." The daughter Shawna was a cute little sparkplug and she said, "No you don't, my buns are really big!" My buddy said, "I still want two buns." Shawna replied, "No you don't – have you ever seen my mom's buns?"

WAIT FOR IT!

I said, "Shawna, it's a small town – who ain't?" I dare ya to make that stuff up!

The partners started to buy each other up and it got down to three of us. I finally sold my shares. I was in it for fun, it was fun for a while – but I had other things that needed getting done.

SUNDRE

Rex

So I moved to Sundre and wouldn't you know it, my new neighbor was one of the most interesting men I've ever met. This guy is famous in North America in two circles – raising world class bucking horses and being a world class hunting guide. Rex knew every cowboy and every bucking horse. The only other guy with a memory like that is Hall of Fame rodeo announcer Bob Tallman.

I won't do Rex's story justice but I'm gonna tell you some pretty incredible things. Rex was not an educated man, I believe he had grade six and then had to help out at home, but he was one of the smartest men I know. He was one of those guys everyone else would quote: "Rex says this; Rex says that." Having said that, Rex was not a talker – ya had to get it out of him. When I met Rex he was already getting on in years and was great company. I was working in real estate and would often pick Rex up for company in my travels. Rex enjoyed traveling and I know I enjoyed his insight and company.

I'll start by telling you about Rex's son Gary. Gary was just starting to enjoy success as a professional rodeo cowboy when he and three others went down in a fatal plane crash. The cowboy community came together as they always do and raised money to search for them. My friend Ivan Daines wrote and recorded a song about it. Trapper Trotter flew countless hours but they never did find them. Their remains were discovered years later by a hiker in the California hills. They were identified by their belt buckles. That took a lot of starch out of Rex.

Another note on Rex: one time he was riding in the mountains, got bucked off and had to ride out with a broken pelvis. This was just another part of what made him a living legend. Now there was never a boast or brag in Rex. In fact, several years later Rex mentioned that incident to me. He asked if I had heard of that and I said I had. He was, "You know they tried to make me out a hero over that – I only did what I had to do. What did they expect me to do? Watch a magpie pick my ass?"

Rex (and I) loved going to rodeos and horse sales. All the guys we liked rubbing shoulders with would be there. Rex was also grandfathered in at the bucking horse sale at the NFR in Las Vegas.

Rex could take five horses and he said to me, "Why don't we take that new truck of yours and haul those horses down there ourselves?" I told Rex my truck wasn't heavy duty enough. Then I ran into an old acquaintance, Ward, who was taking a semi load down. Ward said I have room for five more horses and Rex and you. I relayed this back to Rex and he said, "There's nothing worse than being on foot in Las Vegas, gotta take cabs everywhere. Why don't we just jump in that new truck of yours and drive down." Rex was workin' me tryin' to get to the finals, and I was all in. One thing about Rex was he always paid all of his share and then some extra. I told him we'd split it and off we went. It just may be one of the most interesting trips I've ever been on.

Rex got to visit with all his rodeo buddies. One of his best friends was Butch Small. Another was Rex Bell, who had been the solicitor for the state of Nevada but retired and took over all the legal duties for the Orleans and Gold Coast Casino. So Rex and I got to watch the rodeo on the big screen in the VIP lounge with Rex Bell.

One time I was watching the rodeo finals at my place and Rex at his. This year Cody Ohl was on fire (Rex pronounced it Cody Oil). Cody roped his calf, jumped off his horse, broke his ankle, got to his calf and got him tied. Then he waved for some assistance out of the arena. I thought to myself, "Now there's a tough cowboy."

The next morning I met Rex for coffee. He said, "Did you see Cody Oil last nite?" Yep, I sure did. He said, "Where are they gonna find a tough cowboy – he coulda got himself out of there!" That was Rex!

Now I'm gonna' tell you a story Rex told me. It's a 22 hour pull to Las Vegas from Sundre so we had plenty of time to visit. I had just finished reading a book called "The Rat River Trapper" and after I tell you what Rex told me you will realize that the book is full of lies.

There were songs written over this event and even a movie made in 1981 called "Death Hunt" starring Charles Bronson as Albert Johnson, the man they think is the "Mad Trapper of Rat River" and Lee Marvin as the RCMP officer pursuing him.

The book is supposed to be the official account of what happened in the Northwest Territories when they were taking census counts. They confronted Albert Johnson and he fired a shot and told them to go away. They did but came back several days later and had another confrontation. There were shots fired and RCMP officer Edgar Mullen was shot and killed. Later there was a second fire fight and another RCMP officer was shot and killed. This started the biggest manhunt in Canadian history. It lasted over a month across the Northwest Territories and the Yukon. It was the first time air reconnaissance was used, with First World War pilot Wop May flying the plane. At one point Albert Johnson put his snowshoes on backwards and sent the posse the wrong way. Thirty well-provisioned men chased him across the frozen north, finally catching up with him when the plane spotted him in the open as he was crossing Eagle River.

They shot at him – he shot back – they shot him 26 times. He was so emaciated no one could identify him. There is your official story.

Now anyone who knew Rex knows that he would never lie, boast or brag or mislead. Also Rex has zero skin in the game – not a single thing to benefit from this.

Here is what Rex told me: he made hay with Albert Johnson the next year. Albert simply walked over the McKenzie Mountain range and got away.

Now ask yourself this – why on earth would you shoot a man 26 times? Anyone who has spent time up north knows you can hear bush planes coming for miles, and avoid them. What simply happened was this – the posse came upon an innocent man with his whole winter work on his back. They shot at him. He shot back. Then they shot and killed an innocent man and started the biggest mystery cover-up in Canada. When you read the original book now it will make no sense. The RCMP don't always get their man.

I always wondered just what I should do with this information that Rex gave me – maybe this is it.

Rex left us a couple of years ago. A mutual friend, eight-time Canadian Champion bareback rider Dale Trotter, gave the eulogy. It was the most uplifting, humorous send-off I've ever been at! Rex would have laughed.

Travel in' Cowboys

Whenever I'm with my kids and their little cousins I always try to put a little fun in it. Turns out all kids are way more behaved when they are having fun than when they are being disciplined. I am so glad I was never involved in the "children should be seen not heard" generation. The very opposite end of that spectrum is a pain in the ass as well.

I would tell the kids when we were traveling that we were "traveling cowboys" and could have whatever we wanted when we stopped. What the heck they're nine years old – they wanted a fudgesicle – but it made them feel special. This finally backfired on me. My brother sent his 10-year-old son up to Canada from California on a plane. The stewardesses looked after him on the flight and did a "hand off" to me in the Calgary airport. My sons are several years older at this time but they all really enjoy each other's company! It's funny too how really well behaved kids are when their parents aren't around. Whenever we have little gents, I always do the same thing – I first show them where their nest will be for the night cause sometimes they don't need to be put to bed but would rather slip away by themselves. But then I tell 'em we can have popcorn and watch a movie. Now my little nephew was in heaven. Hanging around with his big cousins – it was like being on a big camp out. Now my house is a little different, having hunting trophy mounts everywhere, a real eyeful for that kid. He politely asked, "Where should I put my shoes?" My son said we don't care what you do with 'em – you can sleep with them on if you like!

Little Rourke was grinning – anything goes.

Now the next day was when I had to learn a lesson. We stopped to gas up on our journey to Saskatchewan heading to the legendary Radisson Fair. I said to Rourke, when you're traveling with just us cowboys you can have whatever you want in there (you know – like a fudgesicle). Well here the little bugger picks out this great big $600 box of fire crackers! I figured serves me right – but hold on, that's not such a bad idea, and I know my brothers would pitch in on the cost anyways. Worked out very well!

This next little story involves my brother in Hong Kong and Rourke's twin sisters. My brother in Hong Kong bought a beautiful pontoon boat for his lake house in British Columbia. He asked Rourke's dad to haul it out there for him. Now Lawrence has always been a real stickler for details and that may be one of the reasons things work out very well for him and why he's so successful. Me, not so much. He told Blair make triple-sure you have a 2 7/8-inch trailer ball to tow it with as Blair had zero experience towing anything. So I volunteered my expertise. Now I have but a slim chance at getting anything over on Lawrence because he has what he likes to refer to as "Spider Senses," but I have a chance if I go through Blair. So Lawrence is coaching Blair to coach me to make sure about the right-size hitch. And I tell Blair that Lawrence is a worrywart and I have a trailer hitch that will work just as well, we don't have to buy another one – trust me. Now, anyone who has ever trailered anything knows this – you use the right-size hitch or you are in real trouble.

Anyway, I would have loved to be a fly on the wall when my message was being relayed back to Hong Kong. It didn't take Lawrence that long to figure out that his leg was being gently tugged.

Now for the boat haul. It's about a six hour trip to the lake and there are two car loads of us heading out there in tandem. We are to pick the brand new boat up from the salesman about halfway there. My brother's 11-year-old twin girls and their friend are riding with me, sitting in the back seat of my truck doing what 11-year-old-girls do (do you know they speak Martian?). I was informed that the twins did not want to be referred to as "the twins" anymore – we want you to use our names – I said, "OK, I'm fine with that – what the hell are your names?"

We get to the rendezvous where we pick up the boat and I start planting the seeds for my next little trick. I say to the girls, "Holy Mackerel, this is a big big boat; I wasn't expecting this! We should be alright, though! It's a big boat!"

We get on the road and things are fine. I mention the size of the boat again and I tell the girls, "We don't have to worry – just as long as we're not on the road with the rock tunnel!"

Guess what's coming just up ahead? We come around the bend and there she is! At first you can cover the tunnel up with your thumb. I say, "Oh boy, there's that tunnel!" And I curse under my breath. I got those kids' attention now! I turn back to them and say, "Listen kids, you hold on tight – I'm not turning back – we should be fine." Away we go through the tunnel, those girls are holding hands together – we get through and travel for a little while. Heidi finally said, "You were tricking us all along, weren't you!" Busted! Hehehe.

Gunshot, Oceanside California

One of my brothers and his wife and four little kids moved to Rancho Santa Margarita, California. A truly beautiful place, rolling hills, near the ocean, but that's also where they can have bad brush fires and mudslides.

Myself and my four sons and one nephew drove down there to visit them. A great holiday! One day just us big guys whom I just mentioned went to this lovely oceanside bar for lunch. We were entering the side entrance when we heard quite a loud "bang" coming from the street/patio side.

My oldest son said, "Dad, that's a gunshot!" I remember thinking I gotta get these hillbillies out more! "No, son, we're not back in the woods now, that's more than likely a car backfire." We got in the restaurant and just nicely got seated when a waiter comes in from the patio on his belly, hollering, "Get down, get down, get against the wall." Now you have all the information we had.

It started utter panic. Everyone did what the waiter said – they got under the table and against the walls. I saw no danger whatsoever and looked at my oldest son and said, "The hell with this." We got up and got out the way we came in. I was not going to do anything really dumb but I was not going to look up at a mad man with a gun from under a table either! We were against the side of the building and I was looking around trying to spot this gunman, but I couldn't see a damned thing. There was a good reason for that, there was nothing to see. The waiter had got it all wrong!

What really happened was simply this: a guy stopped at the stop sign right by the patio, pulled out his pistol and shot the top of his head off! But nobody knew. That waiter assumed there was a gunman on the loose! But you couldn't see the guy in the truck – he was slumped over.

As we are still on alert looking for a mad gunman a police car shows up, then another, then another and then 30! The cops all started getting out and getting their pistols out.

Two cops approached the vehicle while the rest of 'em provided cover. They had their pistols drawn and were taking one step at a time – slowly! They got to the truck, opened the door and dragged this guy out on the pavement with one of the cops keeping his pistol right on him. Then the ambulance showed up and they tried to revive him a bit – keep in mind this guy was deader than a mackerel and didn't have the top of his head! The restaurant had emptied out now – there were over 60 people – and I remember this guy started taking charge now – go figure – there were two young teenage girls crying and he said, "Are you girls going to be OK?"

He turns to me and says, "Are you going to be OK?" Before I could think or craft my words I said, "I'm OK, just one less idiot." I regretted that as it was pretty harsh – but I doubt I'll need therapy. I asked my crew: Are you guys OK? – Yeah, we're fine.

OK, let's find another restaurant. That's one of those things you don't see every day!

So I Wrote, Recorded and Performed a Rap Song

I was helping out with the announcing duties at the Sundre Pro Rodeo – something I really enjoy doing. It's the second best seat in the house – the best being that of the pick-up man. Watching the pick-up men do their job is my favorite part of the rodeo.

I've had the good fortune to meet and become good friends with very likely the best rodeo announcer of all time, Mr. Bob Tallman of Parker County, Texas. Now Bob is not originally a Texan, but he got there as quick as he could. A true gentleman, Bob has the best memory of anyone I know. Every event statistic or even experience Bob had tucked away in his noggin and can recall it at just the right time. More on Bob Tallman later.

Anyway, back to the rap song. I was to go to the local radio station and do a promo for our rodeo. So I went in and gave the dates, times, stock, etc. The usual information. Then started driving home I thought, you know, I can do better. So this rap song popped into my head and I drove back and recorded it in two takes. It was very popular for about three days, only for the fact that no one could believe their ears!

The guy who ran the radio station is a friend of mine named Dan. Dan has a truly unique announcing voice himself and does rhe announcing for the chuckwagon races. He commissioned me, saying, "Do you know what it's called when you mix Country and Rap? It's called 'Crap.'"

They say you don't regret the things you do but the things you didn't do. This one is borderline:
"Rodeo fans get up and clap
To a tune I call the Sundre Pro Rodeo Rap
We're gonna ride some bulls and dog some steers
While the fans in the stands are drinkin' Budweiser beers
Pretty girls chasing barrel and some saddle bronc
Saturday nite we're gonna honky tonk!
T.C. and Company will be the band
Grab your sweetie, take her dancing it will be just grand.
June 22, 23, 24 there'll be fireworks, a midway and so much more.
So don't be shy get up off that chair!
It's the Sundre Pro Rodeo, I'd like to see you there!"

So My Cell Phone Got Stolen

Every time me and my four boys get together there is usually some kind of incident. This time we are in Vegas at New Years going to see Kid Rock. I'd been to Vegas before with two of my sons when we moved my brother and his family there. His company paid for the move and another brother and I were paid to drive his vehicles down, put up in the Las Vegas Hilton and given plane tickets back to Calgary. Two of my boys were available to go, but they didn't get to fly home (they were about 13 and 15). I stuck a $100 bill in each of their socks and they had a 36 hour bus ride back – more on this later.

Earlier we had gone to the "All You Can Eat" seafood buffet in the casino and it was just great! Now my brother Mitch is always pulling pranks on my boys (and on all of his other nieces and nephews, for that matter). This time I see my two sons standing up eating near the buffet line. I go over there and ask why they don't come and sit down. The reply, "Uncle Mitch says they can't charge us if we don't sit down."

So the buffet was just great and those two boys told their other two teenage brothers about all the crab legs and shrimp you could eat, and you know how that goes – always sounds much better than real life.

Oh, back to their bus trip home. I guess they spent too much time with their scamming Uncle Mitch because on one whistle stop on their 36 hour ride home there was a motel. My son goes to the gal at the desk and says, "We need two more pillows fer room 6." She gives him two pillows and he gets back on the bus.

We have a ball touring Vegas and we are going to re-enact the seafood buffet, this time with the whole crew sans Uncle Mitch. The buffet isn't open yet so we sit at the island bar and the bartender is busy setting up for the night. My son puts $5 in the bar gambling machine and is trying to order a drink. The bartender is busy and trying to ignore the kid and finally breaks down, takes the order, and brings him a drink – and he's grouchy.

"That will be $5," he says.

My son says "I'm gambling; I get free drinks!"

"You only put $5 in that machine, I'm not giving you a free drink."

So it goes and I stay out of it. Shortly after my son asks to borrow my phone, which I lend him. Shortly after that the buffet opens up and we get in line. We get in, get seated and I say, "Give me my phone back." He says, "I did." I say,

"I don't have it!" He says, "I put it right next to you." I say, "@*#! that's not giving it back!"

Now I go back to the grouchy bartender and ask for my phone.

He says, "It's not here."

I say, "Well yes it is and I really can't be without it, it has all my contacts, my notes, even my plane tickets."

"It's not here."

Well I know he has it. There was not a soul around but us. I thought afterwards that I should have called it, but he probably would have been ahead of me and turned it off. I can't grab the jerk and beat it out of him or I'd be in jail.

I go to the security desk and tell him what I just told you. He comes over and politely asks for the phone and gets the same result I got. I say let's show the jerk on the security cameras and the guard explains that most of those cameras are dummies – they aren't interested in a little island bar, they are for the card cheats and bigger fish.

I was about in panic mode but thought, you know, I'm not going to let this ruin our vacation – we seldom get together that much.

Unbeknownst to me my oldest son phoned my phone and left a message saying that there was a $400 reward for my phone and not too long after that my phone phoned him back and told my son when and where the exchange would take place.

The next day my son (still without my knowledge) met with two masked men in a vacant lot. He handed the masked men a wad of balled up one dollar bills and they wiped off the phone and gave it to him.

I was never so happy to see him walking in our hotel room in the morning with my phone. He told us of his escapade and how it played out. Now my oldest son is a big guy and not to be messed with. I asked him why he didn't "Hoe it out of them.'" He said it looked pretty dicey. I'm glad he didn't!

So pretty obviously the bartender sold my phone – the jerk. "What do you get when you cross a bartender with an elephant?"

A thief that doesn't forget!

Texas Bound

I love old sayings and they are all said for a reason. "I wasn't born in Texas but I got here as soon as I could" is one of my favorites. I was offered a job to build a water pipeline in the Barnett shale national gas field north of Weatherford, Texas. The job started with first getting permission to move water from one watershed to another. To paraphrase Mark Twain, "Whiskey is for drinking and water is for fighting over!" No truer words than that in Texas. More on the job later.

It was the happiest of times, it was the saddest of times. I was pretty dern sad because I was leaving my boys and other family but also because we had just, and I mean just, buried my mom two days before. Needless to say I bawled all the way to Texas. But don't get your hanky out for me just yet. I was heading off to a great new adventure. The experiences and good friends I was about to have and to meet lay ahead and I keep in contact with them to this day.

Right at the outset, though, I was beside myself. I didn't know how to start. I was always pretty good at decision-making. I would do it like the doctors on the TV show MASH. They would use "triage," which is doing the most critical thing first, then what is next important and lastly what can be put on hold. But I couldn't even decide how to pack. How do you put 50+ years of your life in a suitcase and go? The elk head can't come! My cousin Laurie came out and got things sorted out for me. Number one, there were a whole bunch of decisions that simply did not need to be made then and there – they could be put on the back burner. The fog cleared and it was simple – three pairs of socks, three pairs of shorts, some pants and shirts and get in the truck.

This was the first part of December and the roads were pretty darned icy. I made it as far as Lewiston, Montana the first night. Got a room and headed downtown for supper and a beer. I fell in with a good bunch of guys and talked hunting and drank beer most of the night. I got on the road again fairly early and there was not much improvement in the roads. Traveled for a big portion of the day and made 'er to Cheyenne, Wyoming. I did basically the same thing as the night before. I got a room and headed downtown for supper and a beer. I fell in with a good bunch of guys and talked rodeo and drank beer most of the night.

I was two long days on the road and I wasn't half way to Texas. Part of it was bad roads but a bigger part was the pilot. I figured I better quit socializing and stay on my horse longer! The roads did not improve much till the other side of Denver and after then it was clear sailing. I got on Highway 287 and started making some time. I made it all the way to Memphis, Texas and by now it's pretty dark. There is a beautiful old hotel in Memphis right on the side of the highway. I love these historical old buildings and in another life I'm going to make my living restoring them. I pulled in and there is not one soul around. Kinda spooky, really, but then I see a sign saying, "I'm on the second floor working." I go up the stairs (a beautiful old place) and on the second floor is a ballroom, remnants of the 40's and 50's oil boom. Well there was no one there, so I moved down the line.

A ways down was Childress, home to rodeo legend Roy Cooper. I figured I'd pull in, ask around a bit and maybe introduce myself to Roy. By now it's getting a little late. Childress is a town of about 8000 people and there wasn't a light on – it was darker than the inside of a cow! There wasn't a restaurant or bar open. Nothing left to do but hit the trail.

I'm driving down the highway and my limited imagination is working overtime. What the hell is going on, where are the people, what the hell did I get myself into? I get into Wichita Falls at around midnight and check into a motel. The tallest, skinniest man is standing beside the shortest fattest woman I'd ever seen. I figured I just entered a Stephen King movie – too much time alone with my thoughts. I checked in my room, got my boots off, turned the TV on and was about to relax when BANG BANG BANG on the door. What the hell is this – well, I'm not answering the door without my boots on. I peek out of the curtains and here is this wee little old guy pounding on my door! I opened the door and said, "I expected a bigger dog by the sound of the bark." He said, "What are you talkin' bout – you have to move your truck – you parked in the fire lane."

Now the reason for the dark towns and the streets rolled up – that was my first introduction to "dry counties." You may as well hand a sign out, "We got no business and don't want your business." I really have a problem with dry counties. All they accomplish is making their teenagers drive to another county to get booze and then drive back drunk! I finally make 'er to my Texas destination on the fourth day and started my new life.

Starting the Job

Now the company I was with, well, their main job was recycling gas field waste water, and they were good at it. It was new technology but they had most of the kinks out of it. The water pipeline so far was just talk but that's how every project in the world starts. The fellow that was to give me most of my guidance was a long, tall, older Texas gentleman whom I came to admire. He could get a little rough but then I don't consider that a fault. It can be a useful tool to help get the job done. He gave me many useful insights into Texas and Texans and we got along well. The trouble was that the company was doomed from the start and I'll tell you why later. Right now I'll introduce you to some folks.

I was driving home from a meeting and decided to stop in at this little BBQ joint. I'm standing at the bar next to this cowboy-lookin' guy and he seems to be a little pissed off. We struck up a bit of a conversation and that's how I met my friend J.R. I told him I was new in town and he said, "If you like good music and dancing, come down to the stockyards Saturday night and I'll buy you a beer at Pearl's." I don't really know how to explain Texas hospitality, but they treat you like you're in their home when you're there. Well this was just what I needed. A friendly face and, as Canadians put it, someone "to break the ice." So Saturday night I head down to Pearl's Dance Hall – oh, by the way, a little history here – if you remember "Butch Cassidy and the Sundance Kid," in the movie a school teacher ran off with them. In real life it was a whore out of Pearl's Dance Hall. The movie producers thought that was a little too racy at the time.

I remember walking through the door at Pearl's for the first time. It was almost like going from a black and white film to color, but also going back in time. Everyone was dressed to the nines (whatever that means). The music was mostly western swing, the dance floor was full and the politest bunch of folks you could ever meet. I met up with J.R. and his beautiful bride Zelma and they took me in and introduced me around. I was starting to feel a lot better about my situation and Texas. The stockyards area in Fort Worth is like Bourbon Street for cowboys – lots of great restaurants, honky-tonks, and high end western shops of every sort. I love it there – most Saturday nights found me at Pearl's having beer with my friends.

I also met Billy and Pam Minnick. They are kinda Fort Worth royalty. Again they were so open and friendly. Pam, as you may know, was Miss Rodeo America and could still give 'em a run for their money. And Billy is an ole bull rider, he is the Billy in "Billy Bob's." Billy also was running the Northside Rodeo – an amateur rodeo that runs every Friday and Saturday night. Billy, aside from running one of the most famous bars in the world, is a promotional genius. Firstly, if you buy a rodeo ticket you get into Billy Bob's bar for free. Then he does a few things to fill up his rodeo. They line up 30 little kids in the arena and then let out a sheep with a $20 bill pinned to him and let the kids chase after the loot. That also means their 30 moms, 20 or so dads and grandparents are in the stands cheering them on.

Next they line up 30 bigger kids in the arena and let out a calf with a $50 bill on him – well same thing, 30 moms, 20 dads and 20 more grandparents. The guy fills up his own rodeo. And the announcer pulls the same thing every time. As soon as the kids line up in the arena he shouts, "LOOK OUT, LOOK OUT – there's a bull loose in the arena!" – and boy do they scatter. PRICELESS.

Fort Worth Rodeo. This thing is legendary.

The rodeo starts around the middle of January, runs for 22 days, and features 32 rodeo performances, including ranch rodeo, Mexican rodeo and PCRR Rodeo. It is a marathon. The contractor is Neal Gay and one of the announcers is my good ole friend Bob Tallman. I've never been accused of being shy so when I got to the rodeo arena I went down to the rodeo office to introduce myself. I sought out Neal and told him that I and my old friend (and his too) Harv were gonna bid on contracting the rodeo. Neal laughed like hell and said he'd be happy if we'd take it off his hands. Before I go further I gotta say Brad Barnes oversees the whole rodeo and between him and Neal they put on one of the best productions on the continent.

Now I have always admired Bob Tallman's work. You can recognize that "hall of fame" voice anywhere. One of my earlies memories of Bob was when he was getting interviewed from the hospital bed – he'd been bucked off (and I'll have to ask him where) at some rodeo. The gal doing the interview was trying to blame the horse, but Bob would have none of that: "No, the horse was not at fault – it was pilot error." That's a line I have borrowed from Bob many times!

I have been the guest of Bob and his bride Kristen at his ranch in Parker County on Lone Star Road many times and enjoy meeting up with him on the rodeo trail. He usually gives me a shout-out on some horse or my old friends Harv & Rex. Just a word to the wise, though – be careful what you say around Bob. I don't know anyone who can retain that much memory. There have been many, many things said about Bob's announcing abilities – so I ain't gonna bother – all I'm gonna say is when you see Bob at work you are watchin' a guy who truly loves his job. And it shows. See you on the trail, Bob.

Anyway, this is the first time I'm heading to the Will Roger's Coliseum to watch the roping slack. For those of you who don't know rodeo, "slack" is for the bulk of the rodeo contestants who aren't in the performance. I'm not sure where the arena is and a cowboy rig pulls up beside me. I put down my window to ask for directions. That's how I meet my friend eight-time world champ Super Looper Roy Cooper. Now I don't really have heroes but I sure as hell have people whom I admire a great deal, and Roy fits into that category. He said, "Slip in behind us and you'll be there." A world champ eight times over and one of the most gracious, friendly men you'll ever meet. We became friends and he invited me out to the ranch (it may have been more like he couldn't get shed of me). Whenever I had time off I would head over to Roy's and warm up horses or run the chute, untie calves or whatever. Roy has three sons and a daughter. I know one of Roy's proudest moments was when all three boys qualified for the WNFR in the same year. The boys have a lot of their dad's qualities out of the arena also. Tall, handsome, polite men with not an ounce of brag in 'em – they let their actions do the talkin'. One thing I have to mention is their work ethic – if they were house builders they would build three times as many houses as the next guy. Another thing I noticed was their horsemanship. Oddly enough there are a lot of rodeo cowboys who aren't good horsemen. It's getting better, but it used to be as many guys would spoil a horse a year as would make a good horse a year. These guys were well mounted and I never saw any flaws in their horsemanship.

Well, back to work. We were fighting an uphill battle to begin with. Our technology was expensive but there was an application for us. The trouble started with the stock crash. We should have seen it coming, really – natural gas at the time was $14+ a pail and no one was using it, it was abundant and there was a drilling frenzy out there driven mainly by the land owners and the drilling companies themselves. There was no need for a pipeline now so no need for me. I can tell you it was a sad time and about to get worse! I learned something about an old truth: "You can never go back." The reason for that is this: when you go back it's still the same, it hasn't changed nor have the people, except that maybe they have learned to get along without you. What has changed, though, is you!

The End

I'm going to wrap it up now. It's going to be interesting how this little journey is received and maybe you will hear from me again – you know, like Hangover 1, 2, 3 and 4. Nothing left to do now but sit back and let the movie deals and money roll in.

I said before if you aren't in this book I'll get you in the next one. I hope you enjoyed this – did you pick out the two stories I made up?

I'm going to leave you with two more stories. One is really a proverb that is obviously not mine, I stole it from somewhere, but it touched me so much that I want to pass it on to you as a gift.

An old Indian was sitting with his grandson. He said to him: "Inside every man there is a battle that goes on between two wolves. One is evil, it is anger and jealousy, sorrow, regret, greed, arrogance, self-pity, resentment, inferiority, lies, false pride, superiority and ego.

"The other is good. It is joy, peace, love, hope, serenity, humility, kindness, benevolence, empathy, generosity, truth, compassion, forgiveness and faith."

The grandson thought, then asked, "Grandfather, which wolf wins?" Grandfather replied, "The one you feed."

As for the second story, I'm going to let my old friend Albert have the last word. Remember I mentioned my big red horse Bud? Well when I was away in Saskatchewan my neighbor was looking after him. There was a horrific lightning storm up on that ridge one night and ole Bud and several other horses were struck and killed. The ole bugger should have bought a lottery ticket – same odds.

I was feeling pretty sorry for myself – "somebody needed a hug" – and was looking for some sympathy. I phoned up my old friend Albert.

He didn't use a lot or words – he never does. "Well, you gotta look for the good in it to be thankful for."

I can't believe it! Now I told you that this man just doesn't complain but this is ridiculous! I replied, "Albert what in the hell good can you find in my poor ole horse getting struck dead by lightning?

Albert: "You weren't sittin' on 'im!"